WHAT PEOPLE ARE

LESSONS IN SIMPLY BEING

Carol Eckerman shares with us her gripping psychological, family, and spiritual life story in which I expect every reader will find some poignant personal connections. It is brimming with existential and spiritual insights emerging from the process of living through many painful, beautiful and adventurous experiences and relationships with honesty and humility. Over time she found threaded through her life a mysterious, loving, healing Presence that freed her to trust life, relinquish many oppressive fears and securing attachments, and become more fully the person she was born to be. Her story left me inspired to face further into my own life experiences with a hopeful, loving trust, a desire for the truth, and an awareness of the gifted interconnectedness of all life's happenings in the hidden Love that lives in and among us.
The Rev. Tilden Edwards, PhD, Founder and Senior Fellow, Shalem Institute for Spiritual Formation, and author of eight books on the spiritual life.

To read Carol Eckerman's Lessons in Simply Being *is like a warm and candid conversation with a trusted friend. Her account of her spiritual quest toward peace and wholeness is deeply personal, warm, accessible, and highly readable. I couldn't put it down.*
Rev. Margaret B. Guenther, Professor Emerita, General Theological Seminary, and author of *Holy Listening: The Art of Spiritual Direction*

This deeply spiritual memoir will resonate with many women looking for peace within the tumult of family care relationships. Eckerman's insights increase her comfort with herself and her mother as her mother's thinking and memory decline at the end of life. In well-chosen and articulated glimpses of dialogue and revelations, there are fresh hopeful messages for daughters standing by as parents die incrementally.

Lisa P. Gwyther, MSW, LCSW, Director, Duke Aging Center Family Support Program, and co-author of *The Alzheimer's Action Plan: A Family Guide*

The Lessons in Simply Being that have been part of Carol Eckerman's life journey are movingly described in this book. Through her willingness to begin to navigate "myths of control" she was drawn more deeply into herself. As she embraced the path of unknowing, she was invited to abandon herself to a love that seeks to heal, purify and make all things new from the inside out. Her reflections offer a major contribution to how the spiritual journey contributes to the ongoing integration of all life experience into something beautiful for God.

Fr William Sheehan, OMI, Centering Prayer teacher and retreat leader, Contemplative Outreach of New England

For me this memoir operates on two levels. First, it is a beautifully written story of spiritual transformation in Carol Eckerman's life and in her relationships – especially within her family. One of the most moving sections is about the healing that took place between Carol and her mother, despite her mother's dementia. On the second level, it serves gently and indirectly as spiritual guidance for the reader. On that level I can honestly say that it was deeply transformational for me.

Rev. Larry C. Williams, Director, The Pastor as Spiritual Guide Program

Lessons in Simply Being

Finding the Peace within Tumult

Lessons in Simply Being

Finding the Peace within Tumult

Carol O. Eckerman

Circle Books

Winchester, UK
Washington, USA

First published by Circle Books, 2012
Circle Books is an imprint of John Hunt Publishing Ltd., Laurel House, Station Approach,
Alresford, Hants, SO24 9JH, UK
office1@o-books.net
www.o-books.com

For distributor details and how to order please visit the 'Ordering' section on our website.

Text copyright: Carol O. Eckerman 2010

ISBN: 978 1 84694 723 0

A CIP catalogue record for this book is available from the British Library.

Design: Lee Nash

Printed in the UK by CPI Antony Rowe
Printed in the USA by Offset Paperback Mfrs, Inc.

This is a work of nonfiction. What I have recounted is true to the best of my memory and
understanding. Some names have been changed in order to protect the privacy of
certain individuals.
Unless otherwise indicated, the Scripture quotations contained herein are from the New Revised
Standard Version Bible, copyright 1989 by the Division of Christian Education of the National
Council of Churches of Christ in the USA, and are used by permission. All rights reserved.
Excerpt from "A Hole in a Flute" is from the Penguin publication, *The Gift*, copyright 1999
Daniel Ladinsky and used with his permission.
"Fluent" from *Conamara Blues: Poems* by John O'Donohue. Copyright © 2001 by John
O'Donohue. Reprinted by permission of Harper/Collins Publishers and Bantam Books.

We operate a distinctive and ethical publishing philosophy in all
areas of our business, from our global network of authors to
production and worldwide distribution.

For my mother and my children

CONTENTS

Peace is not something you can force on anything or anyone...
Much less upon one's own mind.
It is like trying to quiet the ocean by pressing upon the waves.
Sanity lies in somehow opening to the chaos,
Allowing anxiety,
Moving deeply into the tumult,
Diving into the waves,
Where underneath,
Within,
Peace simply is.

Gerald May

Preface

It was the summer of 1998 when I first dared to think that, after seven years, I was giving birth to something new. My daughter Lisa was living with me while she took courses at a nearby university. In the fall she would start graduate studies far away; but for now, we were sharing a life of daily camaraderie. We cooked and ate together, laughed and shed tears as we recounted the day's events, and in the evenings sat side by side engaged in our own pursuits. There was an unfamiliar lightness to my mood. At first I attributed the feelings to Lisa's presence and to living easily with someone after years of being alone. I ventured to share this "something new" with Lisa and my son Brett, and a few close friends. They, too, had sensed a change. But I kept on tracking my mood, not quite ready to trust the shift.

At summer's end, I drove Lisa to Ithaca to start her studies at Cornell. We crammed the car with her clothes, some furniture and a few prized possessions: two guitars, a prayer rug, three plants she had nurtured since the start of college, and all the books we could squeeze in. She was about to become an agronomist, a researcher in crop and soil science.

A Baha'i family in Ithaca opened their home to Lisa, also a Baha'i, and to me. We spent the next week transforming a long empty attic space with deeply sloping ceilings into an "everything room." We tucked a low futon bed into a small alcove at its far end, under an octagonal window. An air mattress on the floor became my "guest bed." Lisa, the do-it-yourselfer of our family, introduced me to the marvels of a lumberyard and Kmart. A desk, bookcases, and a comfortable reading area took form, as did drawers made from cardboard boxes and a closet on wheels disguised as a piece of art.

When we finished preparing this home space for her new adventure, we treated ourselves to dinner at the famed

Moosewood Restaurant. It was a pilgrimage stop for Lisa, who at fourteen had declared herself an ethical vegetarian living among a pack of meat eaters. We sat at a table under an abstract picture made from pieces of Ithaca shale. Lisa gazed at the menu, entranced by the treasure trove before her. I couldn't draw my eyes away from the shale. I didn't know why. But I was intrigued enough that, even before we ordered, I went to the bar area to find out about the artist. As I returned to our table, I saw the picture's title—"Unexpected Joy." All at once, recent feelings shifted firmly into place, like the pieces of shale. I realized I was living a new life—one aptly described by these words.

The next day, on my way home to North Carolina, I took a detour through the mountains of Virginia, along the Skyline Drive. As I savored my new life and the natural beauty all around, words began to sound within me: "Write a letter of thanks to Lisa for the gift of this summer together. Write the story of how your despair has transformed into joy—for yourself, and as a legacy to your children."

I wrote the letter to Lisa as soon as I returned home. But it was not until the next summer that I began to write what I came to call my "within despair" story. I was about to undergo a serious operation. Though the odds were excellent that I would survive, I decided to write then—just in case. Childhood had left me well-schooled in imagining all that could go wrong: a quiet dinner turning explosive or settling into yet another new school only to discover we were moving again. I wanted to leave a legacy of hope to Lisa and Brett. They had witnessed the black pit from which I had emerged. My story, perhaps more than anyone else's, might empower them should they, one day, sink into darkness.

As I wrote about those seven years, however, I discovered I was writing for me as much as for them. I wrote amidst tears as well as laughter at the surprising twists and turns of my journey. With distance from the events, and grounding in my new life, I could relive what had been so hard at the time and uncover even more meaning. When I read over my transformation tale, I felt like a young child slowly unwrapping a gift more wondrous than anything she had thought to ask for. A heady mixture of delight, thankfulness, and awe filled me. I had never imagined such emancipation possible. I found myself reading and rereading my story in the weeks leading up to the operation. Remembering what I had already lived through helped me trust whatever might come.

Shortly before the operation I gave copies of the story, in sealed envelopes, to Brett and Lisa. "Read it only if you want to and when you want to," I said. Then we embarked together on a week-long hospital stay. Lisa had taken the time off from school to be with me; and Brett, who lived nearby, joined us for part of each day. Once I became alert after the surgery, they began to read me Richard Adams' *Watership Down*—a favorite book I had read aloud to them years earlier. Brett provided voices for the more down-to-earth rabbits and the combative ones like Bigwig ("And now, you bunch of mole-snouted, muck-raking, hutch-hearted sheep ticks, get out of my sight sharp."). Lisa spoke in softer, breathy tones for the visionaries ("We're in for some mysterious trouble.... It feels more like—like mist. Like being deceived and losing our way."). Doctors and nurses, I noticed, lingered during our readings.

Eight years earlier Brett had eagerly moved away from home to attend Antioch College in far-away Ohio. But when I mentioned the operation, his first words were: "I'll move back home. Don't try to talk me out of it, Mom. I really want to do this." I accepted his offer and rested in his care for the several weeks before I could manage on my own, thankful for his earlier stints as a short order cook and caterer's assistant.

Once assured of my recovery, Lisa and Brett both chose to read my story. They, too, found in it hope and reasons to trust. And sharing the writing brought another gift; we talked together about how each of us had experienced those years. We brought into the light some of the darkness we might have been tempted to hide.

I thought my writing and the birthing of new life finished. Little did I know how much more was to come.

Where to begin the longer tale? I have to start earlier than where I first started writing, earlier than despair transforming into new life. Why the despair? What did I have to learn and unlearn? And why was joy unexpected?

To answer, I must start with the fears and the lessons about living I drew from my childhood—lessons about how to allay or control fear. I lived by these myths of control, largely unconsciously, for most of fifty years. And with them, I constructed what I thought was a pretty good life—wife, mother, university professor, and researcher of infant behavioral development. Only when that life shattered around me, did I begin to capture the old lessons in words and examine them closely.

As new lessons took hold in my life, I felt the grip of the old loosen. I began a journey I had never imagined possible. It led through much of what I had always feared and yet gave rise to a series of emancipations and to a single new lesson to live by.

Part I: Myths of Control

Old Fears – Old Lessons

When my "good life" collapsed, two scenes kept bursting into consciousness. In the first, a child is caught and struggling within a whirlpool that is drawing her inexorably toward its vortex. I do not know when, or how, I first learned of whirlpools; but I can easily imagine fear at a toilet's flushing or my very young self alone in the bathtub, frantically clinging to its rim as I stare at the water disappearing down the drain in a turbulent swirl.

I do remember, vividly, riding as a five-year-old in the front passenger seat of our aging car, eyes riveted to the hole in the floorboard beneath my dangling legs. I watched the pavement race by and felt the wind circling my legs, hands clutched tight to my seat lest I be sucked into this terrifying hole. I now know the whirlpool image represents my terror of being alone and overwhelmed by the strength of sadness, anger, fear…and of being pulled deeper and deeper into these feelings—perhaps into non-existence. These fears had accompanied me for decades.

In the second scene, a solitary child stands in the dark, nose and hands pressed flat against a window, looking in upon a brightly lit scene—a family sitting around a table sharing food, laughter, and conversation. This I came to realize represented my deep longing for loving human companionship and my dread of being shut out from it.

These suspicions, coupled with a childish belief in my own power, shaped the lessons I drew from childhood. In my fifties I captured them in words:

Lesson 1: Life is not to be trusted. Hard things keep happening to you and those closest to you.

Lesson 2: People are not trust-worthy. Your needs increase their fear, anxiety, or anger and make them more self-absorbed and unable to see you, know you, or help you. Only you can help yourself.

Lesson 3: Hide all the parts of you that could possibly bother others. Work to head off or alleviate others' distress.

Lesson 4: Your actions determine how others feel about you and if they'll attend to you. Actions carry value. Your intentions, desires, thoughts, emotions—who you are—do not. Therefore, achieve.

Lesson 5: Males are more important than females. Find a man to love and care for you and you will feel safer, less lonely, and more lovable.

Lesson 6: Do not feel sorry for yourself; others have it harder. Suppress or deny troubling emotions. Just grit your teeth and keep working. Keep doing.

How did I come by these lessons? What gave them their power? And why did I cling to them for so long? Even now, almost twenty years after embarking on this journey of emancipation, why do remnants of these childhood lessons sneak up on me in new guises? I needed to look again at the childhood I'd tried to escape.

Origins

No matter how hard I try, I can recall surprisingly few memories of my life before high school. Only in my late forties did I begin to puzzle about this paucity. Before then, if anyone asked about my childhood, I would just shrug and say something like: "We moved around a lot and that wasn't much fun. But otherwise, everything was just fine."

In my forties, however, I felt overwhelmed, worn-out, by my efforts to keep life running smoothly for me, my parents, my husband Dave, and our two children. Dave convinced me, despite my protestations, to see a therapist with him. After months of talking about how he and I might share more of the managerial duties, I remembered a memory and felt brave enough to mention it.

I recalled how, when I was ten, Mom started having periodic bouts of back spasms that immobilized her for a week or more at a time.

"I was kept home from school for the week," I said. "Mom lay on the couch, and I took care of her and my brother. I cooked the meals, washed and ironed the clothes, and cleaned the house." I felt proud, recounting all I had been able to do.

"Did anyone thank you?" the therapist asked.

"No," I whispered, surprised by my answer and by tears. "I have no memory of ever being thanked."

After several moments of silence, I found myself thinking out loud: "Nobody seemed to see me, my hopes or needs, no matter what I did."

At age forty-seven, I was finally acknowledging that my childhood hadn't been "just fine" — that I hadn't been able to make it "just fine."

Later I remembered a scene with my daughter, she was probably nine, which helped me understand this sense of not being seen. Mom and Dad were sitting in the living room with Dave, Brett, Lisa, and me. After a half hour or more of talk, Lisa suddenly broke into the conversation.

"Hey folks, I'm here, too. Look at me."

Mom and Dad's focus, when drawn outward, centered on males, in this case my husband and son. Males were important and interesting, the people to be looked at, asked about, listened to—and thanked. I felt stung that I had contributed to this pattern of inattention, so familiar to me, by not insisting that Lisa be included.

After the incident with the therapist, I started to reconstruct a picture of my early years—from the few stories told over and over at family gatherings, from memory, and from a handful of probing conversations with my parents. Knowing more about my childhood might help me understand why I worked so hard, why I thought so much was up to me.

I gleaned clues about the young me from the boxes of disorganized photos in my parents' attic. I made a chronological album showing me beside houses that might have been ours, sometimes with people I didn't recognize. I included all the pictures I could find of the young me at family gatherings. Then I initiated talks with Mom and Dad, the only adults still in my life who had witnessed my early years. They were not eager to talk, and they too had trouble remembering. But with the album and my few memories as prompts, we managed to construct a story of my childhood. Later conversations with my mother, as she moved through dementia, helped add more details.

"I was totally unprepared to be a parent," my mother told me, in one of our early conversations, "and there was no one to show me how." I was born in 1941 in Jamaica, New York, seven months before the attack on Pearl Harbor. Within a few months, we moved to a coal town in Pennsylvania, pursuing a job opportunity for Dad, a sales position with Sears. It was a wrenching change for Mom, taking her away from her parents and her network of life-long friends. Less than six months later, we moved again, setting in motion a pattern of repeated dislocations throughout my childhood. When I asked Mom and Dad for help recalling all the places we had lived in those early years, only with difficulty were we able to name seven of them (scattered about Pennsylvania, New York, and Michigan). Both they and I knew there had been others. "Those were just very chaotic years and we were very poor," Dad said, with uncustomary candor and a sigh.

As a result of all the moves, I have little sense of place for my early life. Also the repeated uprooting, the poverty, and our small extended family meant that my formative social world consisted mostly of just Mom and Dad, and then a brother who arrived when I was almost four.

I think I now understand how difficult those years were for my parents. Money was scarce. Dad pursued one moneymaking dream after another, only to have each die—selling office equipment or running an ice cream franchise. He often lashed out in anger, blaming others and railing against the world. When there was no money, we lived for short periods of time first with Mom's parents and then with Dad's. But for most of the time, we had no extended family around us and few friends. Mom, especially, was lonely. During her last years, she once remarked wistfully, "If only Dad had been friendlier, life would have been so different."

Adding to the turmoil was the war and threat of Dad's being drafted. By the time I was eighteen months, we had moved again so Dad could work in a munitions factory. Then, just after my brother Bill's birth, Dad was drafted and his TB discovered. We moved in with Mom's parents for his year of treatment—a regimen of rest, healthy eating, and as much isolation from us as possible, since antibiotics for TB were not yet available. When he was declared well enough, Dad went alone to Detroit for a training program with Remington Rand, a major maker of office equipment. Several months later, after he had a secure job, we moved to Detroit to join him. Once again Mom was uprooted from family and friends, now with two young children. "A very traumatic time" were the words she used when talking about the years surrounding our move to Detroit—my years four through seven.

Dad's angry outbursts, I now know, were usually directed outside the family. But they terrified the young me. I saw his reddened face, his veins bulging as he yelled, and his wildly moving arms and felt myself shrinking away into nothingness— just disappearing. Sometimes, I hid under a table or behind the couch.

Mom's fears and worries kept her preoccupied with Dad and the daily tasks of living. I picture her in near-constant motion, flitting from one household task to another, often worrying about what she had just done and redoing it. By the time I was ten I found it much easier to take over cooking a meal rather than help her as she fretted over each step. She seemed small to the young me, much less a force than Dad. In fact she was tiny, just four feet eleven inches tall and petite in all other ways, too. Dad, of solid build and over six feet tall, seemed immense. I envision him planted in place—a potent, unpredictable force.

My earliest clear memory is of being tied to a bed in a dark room—alone, struggling, and crying out. When I asked about this decades later, Mom told me that I was four at the time and delirious with a high fever from the "real measles," not the milder German measles. We were living with her parents then, during Dad's treatment for TB, and Grandma had helped her figure out what to do.

"We tied your arms and legs down so you wouldn't hurt yourself. You were wild—out of your head! We darkened the room to protect your eyes. We left you alone so that you would wear yourself out and give up crying."

Mom went on to describe me as a difficult child. I was too

active. "You fell off your bassinet." I was squirmy and difficult to hold. "I was always afraid I would drop you," Mom said. "And you were so excitable. You raced around and split your head open on the corner of a wall when you were three."

"You frightened me," she added as she ticked off a long list of my activities—knocking myself out when I stood up under a table or holding my breath so long in tantrums that she would have to pour cold water on me when I started to turn blue. "When you were five you wandered far away from home, causing me great distress," Mom said. "And you always got lost when we were in crowds or department stores."

My second clear memory is of standing on the sidewalk outside a downtown Detroit church, frightened and alone, for what seemed like forever. When I asked about this, Mom and Dad recalled that I had been left at the church for long periods at least twice. Dad had dropped me off at Sunday School before going on to some work-related event. He then forgot about me. Only after he had driven home did anyone realize I was missing. I still can easily call up the picture of that dark gray, foreboding church and its empty sidewalk—and imagine my thoughts. Would he ever come back? Didn't they want me?

Mom recounted another story from this same time period, of an event I can't recall. I was almost run over by a car when I tried to cross the road in front of our house alone. "I heard the brakes screeching from inside the house and collapsed in fright on the sofa," she said. When I asked if I was frightened by the near miss, she replied: "I have no idea. I guess you were frightened when you saw what it did to me. You never did that to me again. I think you learned your lesson."

This story of Mom's brought to mind an experience with my five-year-old daughter. Lisa had fallen from the tree house and scraped her stomach on a wooden beam. Both my husband and I responded to Lisa's crying by racing out of the house to her. Dave reached her first, gathering her up in his arms and holding her tight as he crooned soothing sounds. Once assured of her safety, I burst into tears at the sight before me. I felt such gratitude for our being able to console her, and at the same time, such pain at the remembered sense of not being held and comforted myself.

I also learned from Mom that I was a problem in kindergarten. When I changed schools mid-year, due to our move to Detroit, my new teachers noticed that I stuttered and seemed unable to sit still. "Your teachers thought you were nervous," Mom reported. "And in first grade the principal called and asked whether you had St. Vitus' dance" — a neurological disorder characterized by uncoordinated jerky movements of face, feet, and hands. He insisted that Mom have me evaluated at a Child Guidance Clinic. What followed were two years of counseling in parenting skills for Mom and speech training for me. Both ended when we moved again. But by then, according to Mom, the psychologist was pleased with my progress. I no longer stuttered, and I had begun doing well in school.

When I asked about the counseling, Mom could remember little except that the woman had kept asking her whether she really wanted a daughter. "I wonder why she kept asking me that," Mom mused.

All I can remember was the frustration of trying to master one of my speech exercises. I looked into a mirror and tried, again and again, to curl my tongue lengthwise into a U-shape. I just couldn't do it, even after two years of effort. Only in graduate school did I learn that I lacked the genetic makeup enabling this feat.

One night an arsonist torched our garage in Detroit. Fortunately, the fire only scorched the back of our house. "It turned out to be one of a string of fires set by the local fire chief's son," Mom recounted. Our babysitter, a mature neighborhood woman, discovered the fire and carried Bill and me to her home, amidst all the smoke, flames, and firefighters. I can recall nothing of this, but Mom said we both were traumatized. "You became much quieter, and Bill covered entire pages with black crayon for at least a year."

Around the same time, my leg became seriously infected. "I think it was from your sock's dye," Mom explained. "You had run around outside on wet grass without your shoes on." For one whole summer I had to remain still, mostly in bed, with that leg elevated. I thought the illness my fault. I had caused trouble, again.

When I was in my mid-fifties I read *Ellen Foster* by Kaye Gibbons and felt a deep ache of connection with the young girl in the story. One Christmas Ellen labored to make the perfect present for the relatives who were begrudgingly rearing her, hoping to please them. She asked for only the simplest thing for herself (a pack of white paper), but she hoped fervently that her aunt would see what she really wanted and surprise her with it on Christmas morning. The hoped-for surprise never came, and the gift Ellen worked so hard to make failed to please.

Like Ellen, the young me found Christmas distressing. "You worked yourself up into such a state," Mom said, more than once, "that you were sick in bed most Christmas days."

By the time I was seven I suspect I had formed several conclusions about life and how to handle its dangers. If I had been able to verbalize them then, they might have sounded something like this:

Scary things keep happening. Mom and Dad don't see what frightens me, and other folks always disappear before long. It's up to me to take care of myself. Watch out for Dad's anger, or Mom's worrying. Avoid doing things or showing feelings that bother them. Don't ask for what I want—someone to play with, a snack, or being accompanied on my walks to school. Asking doesn't work; it only makes Mom worry more. Help Mom with her tasks and take over as many of them as I can. If I am helpful and pleasing enough, and work really hard, maybe I can make them see and love me.

My conclusions about life, of course, were those of a child—a child's "truth" with all its limitations. But it is that "truth" that lived on in me and shaped my life.

And life did seem to improve after we left Detroit, although family dynamics remained the same. We moved to Delmar in upstate New York to live with Dad's parents until we had money for a place of our own. The eight- and nine-year-old me was impressed by my grandparents' big house and its back yard with an intriguing two-story garage and a garden pond. Grandma, Mom, and I all helped with the chores. Finally, we had plenty of food—even fried chicken and thick white pan gravy every Sunday.

Grandma told me that she and Grandpa had lived in the upstairs of the garage until Grandpa earned enough as a rural mail carrier to build their big house. I found and climbed the hidden stairway to the garage's upstairs. I loved to play house in these mostly empty rooms, dreaming of possibilities for my parents and me.

Dad worked as a salesman, selling typewriters and adding machines. And Mom took a courageous step to bring some financial stability to our family. A home economics graduate of Russell Sage College, she returned to school under a New York State program aimed at quickly turning college graduates into elementary school teachers. I was sent off to a residential summer camp, at Mom's parents' expense. Dad's parents took care of Bill. And after a few months of book learning and no actual experience in the classroom, Mom began searching for a teaching job.

Mom also started a 4-H club for girl homemakers—one of the Detroit counselor's suggestions. Suddenly I had a circle of friends, one of whom lived right next door. Susan and I walked to school together and played on the large expanse of land surrounding our two homes. We hand-sewed our 4-H uniforms, marched in the town's parades, and showed off our sewing and culinary skills at the county fair.

Mom told me that I liked my new school and did well. "You especially excelled in reading," she said. Her reminiscing late in life told me more: "You went wild on a book reading and reporting challenge, handing in many more than your teacher thought possible." Fortunately, Mom knew I had read all those books, and vouched for me. "You always tried so hard," she added. "You were a perfectionist. I don't know where that came from. Not from me. It was just something in you."

The only troubling memory I can recall from this time is of a classmate who died from a lingering illness, perhaps leukemia or cystic fibrosis. All I remember is her being carried into our classroom each day, and then one day she was no more.

I suspect these two years in Delmar reinforced the rules for living I had distilled from earlier years, especially those about how being helpful, undemanding, and hard-working could make my life and my parents' better.

Our next move was to Latham, New York. Mom had landed a job there as a second-grade teacher in a new elementary school. She began a career that would last well into her sixties. Dad continued in a sales job. And the two salaries meant they could buy their first house, in a development of small cookie-cutter structures plopped into the midst of farmland.

But the new financial security came at a cost. Teaching increased Mom's workload, caused more anxiety, and triggered periodic bouts of back spasms. The memory I shared with the therapist and Dave, about my role during Mom's back troubles, came from our first year in Latham, when I was ten. And, as I've recounted, the feelings evoked in that telling launched my efforts to uncover more about my childhood.

Only quite recently, when other Latham memories kept popping into consciousness unbidden, did I realize that in my earlier remembrances I had skipped right over my years ten to fourteen—moving quickly on to high school. Even if Mom had still been alive, I doubt she could have helped me sort out these memory fragments. The more problematic images came from parts of my life I had kept hidden from my parents and from myself.

The elementary school where Mom worked was within walking distance of our house, and she and Bill took off together each weekday morning. But I was bused into a nearby city, to an ancient red brick school for grades five through eight. Not long ago I remembered and wrote about one of my first days at this school:

I'm mortified, crouching in this dark hole, trying not to cry—or scream—wishing I could vanish. It's my first week in fifth grade. I'm sure in another year, there would be no way my body could contort itself to fit in the kneehole of my teacher's desk. A plump woman blocks the way out. I see only her thick ankles and heavy brown shoes. Yet other pieces flash through my mind. A pinched, scowling face. Her eyebrows. I can't forget them. They're higher on her forehead than any I've ever seen. Are they painted on? Her mouth bellowing before settling into a pose of distaste. Her surprisingly strong arms dragging me into this hole—out of sight.

What have I done wrong, again? I have no idea. No one's told me the rules of this school or classroom. I would have obeyed them to the letter.

I imagine the other children sneaking glances and smiling with smug satisfaction. "You're one of the 'country kids,'" two "city kids" had told me earlier. Bused in, uninvited, unwelcome. Worse. I'm not even a "farm kid" but one of those from "the development." I had doubted I could sink any lower in status, but surely I've done it now.

As the minutes drag on, I wonder what comes next. When will she let me out? Will there be more punishment? I'm not sure I ever want to leave—at least not until everyone else is gone. But there's that long bus ride home. I can see no way to avoid it.

Dread grips even harder. What about Mom? When she asks, "Were you good in school today?" what can I say?

I'll have to just say "yes" and not let my face or body give me away. I can't worry her.

The strength and rawness of these feelings, even all these decades later, helped me realize what the Latham years had added to the power of my childhood lessons. I learned that I bothered lots of people, not just Mom and Dad. Although I can remember nothing more of all four years at this school, I suspect a steady stream of "little" events kept reinforcing and deepening my sense that in the eyes of many people, both adults and peers, I was unlikable.

Outside of school, my memories are better: all the ways I helped at home, my skill and freedom in ice-skating on the pond behind our house, my ability to care for the preemie twin babies down the street, and the beautiful foil Christmas ornaments I sold door to door to raise money for our 4-H club.

I now think that "hiding and hoping" became even more a way of life during these years. I hid what I imagined bothered others, and hoped that folks would see the good in me and like me.

One day a bunch of us early adolescents were playing touch football in the street in front of my house, when two teenagers we didn't know appeared. They invited us to join their church's youth group in an affluent town nearby. "Our leader will pick you up and bring you home," they offered. Only I expressed interest. And after Mom talked with the male youth leader, he started ferrying me back and forth.

I found a friendly group that did such fun things as roller-skating at a rink rather than in the street and debating right versus wrong ways to handle timely issues like being kissed. I kept going and started attending their church services and "family nights," too. Folks here talked a lot about how to be good, and I desperately wanted to be that.

This church gave me a taste of "family," of being held within a caring community; yet I always remained an outsider. The youth invited me into their church, but not their homes. The persistent message, "God loves you," nurtured my hope that I was likable; but I also knew that these church folk had sent their youth into my neighborhood because of all they thought we lacked. Despite my pleas, Mom and Dad never came to church with me. On "family nights," I sat in the midst of a family like I dreamt of—the youth leader's—fighting feelings of loss and shame.

Just as I was about to start high school, we left Latham. We moved to Clinton, New York, the home of Hamilton College. In Utica, Dad had a chance to run his own business, selling and repairing office equipment. Mom found a teaching job in Clinton. I often wondered how we came to live in this more expensive town, rather than Utica. Just a few years before her death, Mom mentioned that she had held out for the college town, wanting its educational opportunities for Bill and me.

Mom's determination played a pivotal role in my life even though it did little to change our family dynamics. Dad was still volatile, and Mom worried and remained preoccupied with Dad's turbulence. I hid whatever I thought might bother my parents and kept trying to head off or minimize outbursts. Mom and Dad seemed more interested in Bill's Boy Scout activities than anything I did. Money was found for his uniforms, camping supplies, and trips; whereas my clothes—that bright orange skirt with huge white polka dots—came from Grandma's church rummage sales. Although I had been playing the flute since fifth grade, there was no money for private lessons or an instrument of my own.

But at Clinton Central High School I found I could excel in the classroom and that academic achievement was seen and prized by the faculty. Two female teachers befriended me, introducing me to whole new worlds of conversation. Others encouraged me to express myself in prose, poetry, and music—and to aim high. I recall the woodwind instructor rushing in one day, waving a newspaper article in my face. "You can do this," he exclaimed. A woman had just won the "first flute" position in a major symphony orchestra. With his encouragement I began to practice as many as five hours a day. He, a jazz clarinetist, took me to musical events, encouraging my love of both classical music and jazz. These teachers and others helped nourish in me a deep intellectual curiosity and a belief in my capacity to learn and reason. They also helped me discover my creative abilities and find safe ways to express something of the inner me.

I also became active in the youth group at the local Presbyterian church. I seemed to fit in here just fine, and my parents started attending church with me.

My new teachers and youth group leaders affirmed me— something I so longed for. But I thought their approval and support was the result of my doing, my excelling at tasks. I did not dare link their appreciation to the whole of me.

Some of the skills I had developed at home now served me well with peers. I knew how to reduce others' anxieties, how to remain outwardly calm in difficult circumstances, and how to forestall or minimize outbursts during times of conflict. I also made few demands on others. And my doing, and excelling at doing, led to leadership roles both in school and out.

I threw myself into a wide range of activities: band, orchestra, badminton and softball teams, student council, outdoor girls' club, press club, library club, slide rule club.... By my sophomore year I was a class officer and dating members of the football and ice hockey teams. I was welcomed into the group of reasonably popular students, the group of class leaders, and the group of high academic achievers, among other cliques. But again, I related the affirmation to what I did, not to who I was.

I especially remember and value a friend who invited me into her working-class home. Her family gathered around the dining table each noon for their main meal. I often joined them and witnessed their easy camaraderie—how they listened to one another and cared about what was happening with each member of the family, and with me. They offered a picture of the life I yearned for. Their way of interacting became a model for my own family-to-be.

I remained aware of status distinctions, but now they felt less all-determining. Town kids like me were lower in status than the children of the college faculty, yet I found I could achieve with the best of the faculty kids. The two boys I dated the longest were Catholic. Their priest called each of them in for a conference about the dangers of continuing to date me, a Protestant. My boyfriend and I would discuss these issues, but we kept on dating.

Early in high school I concluded that college was not a goal my parents had for me. Mom and Dad seemed most concerned about my becoming marriageable. Although I was skilled in domestic tasks and I dated regularly, they worried that I was too intellectual. Dad even set himself the task of teaching me to play golf. "It might help you get married," he said. The lessons ended quickly when I embarrassed him by hitting a ball into a group of nearby golfers. Driving lessons ended even quicker. Dad instructed me, my first time behind the wheel, to back slowly out of our driveway. When I hit our garbage pail as I tried to turn into the street, Dad declared: "It's hopeless."

I decided I wanted to go to college, and teachers and friends encouraged me to pursue this goal. College seemed to promise a way out of my home situation and to open up new life possibilities. I never directly asked my parents if they would send me for fear of being disappointed or even prohibited. Dad, who hadn't attended college, often spoke disparagingly about the unwarranted advantages given to college graduates. I decided I would ask for their help only when I had in hand a decent scholarship and a sizable amount of money. So I worked even harder at school to receive merit scholarships; and from the age of fifteen on, I worked every day after school and on weekends. During the summers, I worked full-time in the town library and played my flute in musical groups. As I labored to make college possible, I discovered another plus of excelling. My achievements brought pride and smiles to my parents. They noticed me when I won awards.

In my senior year I entered a speech contest in order to get a flute of my own. I had been using school band equipment and desperately wanted an instrument that would enable me to come closer to producing the music I heard in my heart. All my work money I saved for college. But if I won the prize money offered by the local Jaycees for the best speech on "my true security," I thought I could buy a flute. I did win the local contest—and my flute—and I went on to win at the state level before losing at the national. The closing sentences of my speech capture me well at this point in life. Imagine them said with confidence and zeal:

"Yes, in a very real sense my world is what I make it. If I am content to be just another voice crying, 'Look at this world— injustice, anxiety, tension. There is no security,' then I shall have no security. However if I look life squarely in the face, see a job to be done or a problem to be solved, and on my own initiative, relying on God and myself, do what I can in the situation, then I shall have my true security."

In my late fifties I revisited other memories of my high school years and realized for the first time what an important source of support for my early life I had had in Grandpa—Mom's father. While my other grandparents seemed stern and formidable, I've always had warm feelings for Grandpa. Mom did, too. When she was growing up, her mother took to her bed several times with "nervous breakdowns." Her father took over, caring for the whole family. Mom often talked warmly of one of these times when she was just about to go off to college. Money was tight after the financial losses of the Depression, so Mom's father taught himself how to sew and made all her clothes for college.

I remembered Grandpa taking me to ride the carousels when I was a little girl. He and a partner owned these rides. Grandpa, a skilled carpenter, had built some of them and renovated others. I could ride as many times as I wanted and try, again and again, to catch that golden ring. In my memory, Grandpa is watching me and sharing in my joy.

When I was in high school, he and Grandma made the day-long trip to visit us for a few days every Thanksgiving; and Grandpa always found time to invite me to a walk alone with him. I can feel his hand in mine as we strolled and hear him asking: "Now, tell me Carol, what has been going on with you?" I knew he wanted to know about the whole me and that he cared. He was, I think, the primary person who kept love and hope alive in me. Even today, I smile each time I see his hand-made wooden toolbox that occupies a privileged position in my dining room. Grandpa and that box were inseparable.

By the time I graduated from high school, I had a full tuition scholarship and enough money saved to attend college. I knew how to control or minimize life's dangers, so I thought. And I was eager to leave home and tackle the task of making a good adult life for myself.

Constructing a Good Life

I had pinned my hopes for a better life on going to college. I wanted to explore its new intellectual horizons and educate myself for a rewarding job (I was determined to be able to support myself.). Even more important, however, was finding a man who would see the real me and like me, love me, and want to share life with me. The novels I devoured about women being "saved" by men enflamed my imagination. I had experienced the joy of being affirmed by my grandfather, male youth-group leaders, the flute teacher, and boyfriends. And I had sensed throughout my life my parents' valuing men over women and Mom's clinging to Dad. Clearly, having a man care for me would provide more security and prove that I was of value—indeed that I was lovable. I wanted to find a life partner, a man who would fill the void of aloneness that haunted me.

I met Dave the summer after my first year of college. He was two years older and a student at the college in my hometown. "We met in the adventure section of the Hamilton College library," we told friends. This story was close enough. I was working in the library that summer and he kept coming up to the reception desk whenever I was stationed there. Since we both were working every day and most nights, it was hard to schedule a first date. And we might not have gotten beyond one, except for our senses of humor. One of Dave's jobs was caring for an elderly professor. Dave proudly showed up for our first date in the professor's car, but he had forgotten about the garbage pail he'd left in the rear of this station wagon after an earlier trip to the dump. As we drove along—we were on our way to one of my band concert jobs—the metal can rolled from side to side, creating percussion sounds we had to shout over. We tried to ignore the interloper, but soon succumbed to laughter.

By summer's end I viewed Dave as so much more mature,

intellectually focused, and fun than the other guys I had been dating. I came to believe that he saw and liked important parts of me—my caring for others, my doing, my intellectual curiosity and passions, and the playful nature I had discovered in myself with the help of high-school and college friends.

Our dates that summer were full of pranks. On one, Dave was to bring his friend Bill for a blind date with my friend Julie. Julie and I barricaded my front porch, made its floor shine with water, and posted a "wet paint" sign with instructions to use the other door. Dave and Bill arrived at the back door only to find its doorknob missing. They set out searching for still other ways in. Eventually we ushered them in through the basement. We all had a good laugh and our prank helped relieve the blind date awkwardness.

When I returned to college, Dave and I began to correspond regularly. We met during vacations at each other's houses or in the railroad station as I passed through his hometown on the way to mine. In our letters and times together, I shared more of myself than ever before. Dave saw something of my needs and didn't flee, and he was as avoidant of anger and conflict as I. I appreciated his gentle ways and decided he was someone I would dare to trust. At each parting, words from the Everly Brothers' hit, "Bye Bye Love," sang within me. Here came that loneliness again.

Childhoods that left both Dave and me needing to prove ourselves "good" sheltered us from much of the winds of change of the early 1960s. We were idealistic, but not confrontational. We would work to change existing societal structures—from within.

Dave began graduate studies at Columbia University, in experimental psychology, while I still had two more years at the College of Wooster. I, too, was heavily engaged in psychological research by then. College had opened my eyes to the possibility of using the methods of science to uncover order in human behavior, a dazzling prospect. I had spent the previous summer as a research assistant at Wooster trying to do just this in studies of human learning. So during the next two summers I found a way to work near Dave. As a research assistant at the New York State Psychiatric Institute, a part of Columbia Medical School, I interviewed strangers throughout the parks of Manhattan, asking them to tell me the first word that came to mind after I recited a list of words. It proved quite an introduction to life in the big city—to finding my way about by subway and bus, to experiencing the amazing variety of people and neighborhoods, to sizing up folks for approachability and safety, and to keeping in sight a policeman or someone else who might help if trouble erupted.

Dave and I became engaged during the spring recess of my senior year, while we were visiting at Grandpa's home. Excited, and for once eager to share this news with my parents, I called them. Dad answered.

"Dad, I have big, wonderful news. Dave and I are engaged to be married." The words tumbled out of me.

"You're kidding," he said, bursting my bubble of joy. He wasn't joking.

The next fall I became a student in the same graduate program as Dave, thanks to a National Science Foundation Fellowship. I suppose just being at Columbia then was a form of confrontation. Only three females were admitted to the psychology department's large incoming class, and some members of the all-male faculty refused to allow us to work in their laboratories—because we were women. During orientation our class was told: "Look to your right. Look to your left. Within a year, half of you won't be here." It proved true. And far fewer than half eventually earned a PhD. All three of us women did.

Money was tight. Dave had the cheapest dorm room on campus. For seven dollars a week I rented a room in a woman's apartment. The only drawbacks were the woman's unexplained disappearance within a month and the building's DC electricity that had me holding my head before an open gas oven to dry my hair. We ate at local restaurants whenever they offered beans and franks specials, and we often waited hungrily outside the locked entrance to the Union Theological Seminary cafeteria until some seminarians let us slip in behind them for the three-course meal that cost less than a dollar. We married at the end of my first year of graduate studies.

Both Dave and I did our graduate research on basic learning processes in animals—pigeons and rats. I followed Dave to his first position at the University of North Carolina in Chapel Hill, where a faculty member on sabbatical leave gave me free rein of his laboratory to finish my dissertation research. True to my goal of trying to integrate the fields of animal and human learning, I was training pigeons in a learning task analogous to one frequently used with college students.

At a faculty party that I attended as "wife," I became engrossed in conversation with Professor Harriet Rheingold, a pioneer in the empirical study of human infant development. We talked almost non-stop about our research passions. By the end of the evening she offered me a job as a Research Associate, and I accepted. But I lay awake most of the night, wondering what on earth I had done. The next morning I ran to the library to read all I could of what this woman had written. Just before five o'clock I rushed into her office.

"Were you serious about your offer?" I asked.

"Yes," she replied, "although it kept me awake most of the night. I don't think I've ever done such a rash thing."

We laughed as I confessed my sleeplessness and rush to the library. "But I really want to work with you," I declared. "I like the rigor of your research, your focus on processes of change, and that you are studying the organism I really want to know about— the human infant."

We worked together for five years, studying newly-crawling infants' readiness to explore unfamiliar spaces, objects, and people. We asked how their exploration supported learning and developmental change. Dave's and my first child, Brett, was born during these years—adding more fuel to my passion to understand early development.

I loved the work with Harriet and would have continued had a nepotism dispute not arisen. The chair of the department and the Dean raised questions about the appropriateness of Dave and me working in the same department, even though I was fully supported on federal research grants and did not participate in any faculty meetings or decisions. Once it became clear that fighting their interpretation of the nepotism rules would make Dave's job untenable, I looked for some other way to continue my research.

By now others thought of me as a developmental psychologist—a surprise to me who had never taken a single course in this area. I was offered two near-by academic jobs, as a developmental psychologist. I took the riskier but more exciting one, a one-year Visiting Assistant Professor position at Duke University. Fortunately the gamble led to a regular tenure-track position the following year. Now I was solely responsible for the direction, execution, and funding of my research; and I was teaching Developmental Psychology to a class of 167 students.

I weathered several bumps along the professional road—at first, some male faculty members openly arguing against the hiring of a woman for the tenure-track position (worse, the mother of a two-year-old); then when I gave birth to Lisa two years later, the absence of any maternity leave policy ("It hasn't happened before," my Dean said.); and later, concern that my research was collaborative, multi-disciplinary, and not theoretical enough. For a few years, I was the sole female tenure-track professor in the department. But despite the general sexism of the time, there were men who supported me: Dave most importantly, some of my new department colleagues, and a Duke Medical Center neonatologist and later an Environmental Protection Agency neuroscientist who sought me out for collaborative research—to accomplish something neither of us could do alone.

Dave and I had no models for how to manage two careers and a young family. We made up the "rules" as we went along. We began with a joint commitment to rearing our children well and in agreement that Dave's career took precedence over any job I might have. A big-time career had never been my goal. All I hoped for was some intellectually challenging work that would add value to the world and enable me to support myself and my children if that became necessary.

After Brett was born, Harriet Rheingold gave me a good deal of flexibility. I stayed at home for several months and then gradually resumed working after we found a "housekeeper," an African-American woman who had taken care of several other infants. By the time I started at Duke, Brett was attending a church-run daycare center that accepted children as young as two—one of the few such facilities available then.

Lisa was born during my third year at Duke. Fortunately, even though she arrived two weeks early, she waited until I had just given my last final exam for the spring semester. I did the grading in the hospital, between bouts of nursing. One of my undergrad students, I learned later, won a sizeable amount of money from a betting pool (Would I make it through the semester?). Despite the absence of a maternity leave policy, the chair of my department relieved me of teaching duties for the fall semester—"off-the-books." I still served on committees and spent as many hours as possible in research since the tenure clock kept running. Before Lisa turned four, I would need to have made my mark on the field of infant development to continue at Duke. Our housekeeper cared for Lisa while I worked until she could be enrolled as a three-year-old in a newly-opened Montessori school.

Along the way I made decisions that others thought could only end in career failure. I attended only one professional convention a year and devoted evenings and weekend days to family. Dave spent many more hours at career building than I; and his career steadily progressed, to our mutual delight. When both children were in grade school, we each decided to spend one afternoon a week at home with them after school. A college student provided fun activities the other afternoons. First one and then a second female student took on this role, becoming an honorary member of our family.

Somehow it all worked. Dave's promotions came at the customary times, and eventually I became a Full Professor at Duke. It just took me a bit longer. Our decisions hadn't doomed either of our career paths.

Our marriage worked for me in many ways. I felt seen and cared for, more secure, even lovable. Conflict was rare; and displays of anger, rarer still. Together, Dave and I weathered many difficulties: times of very little money, the rigors of competitive academic life, a series of miscarriages, several operations, serious medical problems surrounding our children's births, and Grandpa's death.

I felt relieved and grateful to have a helpful companion, yet I still carried the image of being caught in a whirlpool that threatened my existence. I drew dangerously close to its vortex when I awoke from anesthesia, crying out for our baby, after a third miscarriage—this time after four months, and after I had dared to believe in this child. And then again, during the terrifying months in which I would suddenly awaken in the night with a racing heart, limbs that tingled, and strange and frightening visual and auditory sensations. Months of tests followed. I tried several medications and had bizarre atypical reactions to each. Finally, after months of slow withdrawal from the final drug, the condition ceased without any definitive diagnosis. As potentially overwhelming as these times were, Dave was with me; his presence made it all bearable. I was not alone in the whirlpool.

It wasn't all hard times. There were many times of joy, smiles, and laughter—and the quiet sense of well-being as we worked together. True to the vision of family life drawn from my high-school friend's family, Brett, Lisa, Dave and I gathered almost every evening around a dining table to share news of everyone's day, to laugh, and to care for one another.

When I think of my joy in this family, one memory keeps reappearing. It is of the weekend evenings spent at our lake cottage after a day full of swimming, canoeing, and other outdoor activities. After dinner we all would gravitate to the living room to spend the evening side by side, each in our own favorite pursuits, with occasional easy conversation. No longer was I on the outside of the window, looking in longingly upon others.

I have a good life, I thought.

With Dave and the children I now had the family I had longed for as a child. I felt seen and loved and cared for. I had a rich intellectual life and rewarding work. No longer did I need to worry about having enough money. The old fears might rear their heads, but I trusted Dave and our ability to handle life together.

Throughout my married years, I remained in regular contact with Mom and Dad through weekly letters and phone calls and twice-a-year family visits. They had moved at the end of my college years to Long Island, across the street from Mom's parents. So for several years, stays with my parents meant welcomed time spent with Grandpa. In the summers, Grandpa and I would row together up and down the salt water Carmen River that led into Great South Bay, talking and examining all the forms of life we came upon. Or we powered up the rowboat's small motor and crossed to Fire Island for a swim in the ocean.

When Mom was ill or Dad hospitalized, I went to care for them. I felt I had brought pleasure to them by bringing these new males—first Dave and then Brett—into their lives. I continued to tell them news about us that I thought would please them and to hide anything that might cause concern. I never told them about my three miscarriages and two operations. I did not want to deal with the anxiety this news would trigger in Mom. When Dad railed in my presence, I found a way to leave the room. I still followed all the old lessons in my interactions with my parents.

In my forties, my brother Bill and I forged a new relationship. We had never been very close as children. I resented my parents' preferential treatment of him, and he didn't appreciate following after me in school—being known by teachers as "Carol's brother" and expected to be as high an achiever. After college we lived far apart and saw each other only infrequently, usually at Mom and Dad's home. But when Bill, following a job opportunity, moved with his wife and son to a town less than an hour away from me, we began to enjoy having Easters, Thanksgivings, and Christmases together as well as the occasional everyday evening. It helped, too, that our children were delighted with their cousins. The Christmas gatherings in my home with Mom, Dad, Bill and his family brought me closer than ever before to experiencing the family of origin—and the holidays—I had longed for. I was thrilled when Mom remarked, "What a lovely Christmas this has been."

I had life under control, so I thought.

Part II: Within Despair

The Good Life Collapses

As I approached my fiftieth birthday, the life I had worked so hard to construct started to shatter about me. The man I had pinned my hopes on said he had to leave me, after twenty-seven years of marriage. It happened suddenly, without warning or explanation. All Dave could say was that he was confused and unhappy with his life.

"I don't know what I want, but I need time to be by myself and try to figure this out. I hope you will stay put, give me time and space, and wait to see how it all turns out."

At first I was numb and in shock. But then the despair began—at the threat of abandonment by the person I had trusted and depended on to make life livable. Dave had been mother, father, lover, husband, and best friend to me. Now it was as if they all could die at any moment, only worse. As they died, they would be rejecting me. The old feeling of shame, of not being "enough," returned full force. Had Dave ever cared for me at all? If so, how could he hurt me so much? Was I really unlovable? Was no one trustworthy? These questions held me in almost unbearable suspense.

I felt great sorrow for my children, too. I had let Brett and Lisa down terribly. Our loving, nurturing family was collapsing.

I was alone and struggling within the whirlpool I had always dreaded. Despair, fear, and sorrow might have overwhelmed me completely had I not known at a primal level that I would continue to support my children's lives. This need and desire was a lifeline. I clung to it. I knew I wanted to live until Lisa and Brett were at least in their thirties. I would survive each day for them and decide later if life were livable.

I decided to do what Dave asked—stand in place, ready to resume our life together if that was what he wanted. I reverted to following all the old lessons with him. I tried to be caring, undemanding, and helpful despite my distress. If I were "good" enough, maybe Dave would once more want to share life with me. I discovered, however, the perils of "staying put." I felt I could not talk freely to anyone about what was happening and that I could take only the smallest steps to create new supports for life.

The "keep doing" lesson seemed to serve me well. I reacted to despair by becoming even more active. Whenever I could find a break in work or home tasks, I walked—several hours most days. Sheer physical activity helped get me through the day.

I struggled to find some human companionship for Lisa and me. Brett was a day's drive away from home, in his second year of college; but Lisa was still living with me, a sophomore in high school. My parents couldn't help. Mom simply advised, "Be sure to eat well and get a lot of sleep." Dad withdrew and refused to talk. His behavior looked to me like anger, and I couldn't tell who the target was—perhaps me. Shame distanced me from my few friends at work. I felt I couldn't tell them what was happening, that I needed to hide my distress. Bill and his wife Shirley reached out to us, but their questions and comments added to my distress: "Why did Dave leave? Was it because of your career, your earning more than him?" "It isn't fair."

So I reached out to Lisa's school, a Quaker community. I spoke to the teachers closest to Lisa, enlisting their help for her. Just being able to tell someone what was happening to our family was a relief.

I also remembered how, in my youth, church groups had provided some sense of family. Although my church-going had ceased when I entered graduate school, I now visited two churches in search of a home. These first tries were disastrous. I sat alone, knowing no one, feeling more cut off from human companionship than ever. I left in tears. I made one more attempt; but this time I talked with the pastor first, to ensure there would be at least one familiar face at the service. I began to visit this Presbyterian church regularly, in large measure because I thought the pastor was dealing courageously with his own personal crisis—over a progressively debilitating neuromuscular disorder.

Two months after Dave's leaving, I became aware that Brett was struggling with personal problems unrelated to the marital crisis. He decided to drop out of college temporarily, join Lisa and me at home, and undergo counseling here—the decision I had hoped for. But his return added to the chaos of home life. All three of us were struggling to understand Dave's departure. Why? What did it mean about us? What was happening to this family? I had no answers for my children, or myself; and the uncertainties took their toll daily. Despite my efforts to appear strong and hopeful, the kids saw my pain. They wanted to help, but how? Brett's crisis added to our pool of sadness and confusion, and left Lisa and me struggling to understand and help him. Also, after the relative freedom of college life, Brett chafed at our old routines. What new ways could we find to live together?

Dave and I spent a few tense hours together most weeks. Our meetings had me striving to be understanding, patient, and everything else he wanted—without knowing what that was. I now realize it was a no-win situation, but at the time I thought everything for our family depended on each of my looks, words, or gestures.

Despite the agony of these months, I experienced some good things. Most evenings I sat near Lisa as we went about our separate activities. What began as a conscious attempt to help her feel my love, quickly showed me how much she gave back. Her quiet presence, smiles, and hugs reminded me that I still had love in my life.

Prior to Dave's leaving, I had been immersed within just two worlds: my family and the competitive, predominately male academic world in which I worked. I am embarrassed to admit how surprised I was to find in the church several people who seemed genuinely caring and likable. I joined a group of folks who were considering formal membership. We met for six weeks with the pastor and then later, monthly, just to enjoy each other's company. This was the first friendly, supportive group I had been part of since graduate school days. It dawned on me—very slowly—that some of these people liked me, even though I was so often sad and in no position to help them. I started to make a close female friend, a first since college.

Amidst the turbulence at home, Brett, Lisa, and I took steps toward renegotiating our relationships. One scene stands out as illustrative of the good changes. I overheard Brett and Lisa talking—arguing really—at the kitchen table. I don't remember the exact topic but it probably was something that had been discussed at Lisa's school that day, perhaps the role of the UN or ways to work for social justice. Back and forth they went: Lisa presenting her idea; Brett who had always been the more forceful, opinionated child negating her view and presenting a counter argument; Lisa defending her view. On and on, in the long-standing pattern.

But then I heard Lisa say in a firm but quiet voice: "It doesn't matter what you say, Brett. I know what I think and why. Nothing you say will change that."

In the dead quiet that followed, I peeked into the kitchen and saw Brett's surprised—shocked—face.

A few hours later, Brett found me alone. "What's happened to my little sister, Mom?"

I explained how Lisa had blossomed into her own in high school, and during this time as the only child in the roost. Nothing more needed to be said. From that day on Brett and Lisa nurtured a new relationship, one of mutual respect and learning from each other. They would become close friends.

And I started talking about our more explosive days as the consequence of our being "emotionally labile." In time these words—so professorial, so Mom-like—became able to elicit a smile or even a giggle from one or more of us and diffuse the tempest.

When family dynamics, my own turmoil, and the demands of professional life finally overwhelmed me, I asked Dave for some relief from always being the one who was "on" with our children. He took over in my home one evening a week, giving me a few hours for myself and Brett and Lisa more time with him.

After Brett's life became more stable, Lisa and I did take one giant step. We traveled to Belize with a group from the church to live for two weeks in a Mayan village. We worked side-by-side with the villagers, building a primary school. Here were clear challenges that we could meet and enjoy: living and eating simply, sifting pebbles from the sand we gathered from a river bottom in order to make mortar, and learning to construct cinder block walls. And we basked in the strengths of this village community. Electricity had yet to reach the area, but their homes and churches stood open to us long into the night. Wherever we went, we found cut flowers gracing the humble space, warm hospitality, and people ready to engage and teach us. After several aborted attempts and good-natured ribbing, I mastered the art of making tortillas on their wood-fired stoves. Lisa and other teenagers in our group joined village youth to lie in a field beneath the stars, late into the night, sharing dreams and hopes.

Only much later did I realize what a valuable lesson these villagers had given me about a decidedly experiential way to teach and learn. When the time came to help build the walls of the new school, men from the village took their places on either side of me. Without a word, one met my eyes and then with exaggerated, slow movements spread the mortar along the top of the partially-constructed wall. He then handed me a block with a glance toward the mortar. I laid the block upon the mortar, very carefully, only to have my effort met with a gentle shake of the head. One of the men removed my block, smoothed the mortar, looked at me and slowly set the block down. The whole sequence was repeated once, twice, three times before I finally placed the block just right. Then smiles and a bit of laughter all around. Next, one handed me a trowel and by gesture invited me to spread the mortar. Again smiles, removal of my attempt, another slow patient demonstration, my turn.... Within an hour or two, I was on my own and reasonably proficient—without a word being exchanged. No questions by me, no verbal instructions or corrections. Just looks, smiles, gestures, and patient demonstrations. I began to see just this kind of teaching and learning everywhere in the village, especially among the children who daily ringed our worksite.

Ever since childhood I'd been attentive to my parents' nonverbal cues, but as a defensive strategy, a way to ward off difficult emotions. As my father began to scowl, I might say, "Have some more chicken, Dad," forcing a smile. With the villagers, though, I delighted in our openness to one another's facial expressions and gestures. I didn't need to be cautious or hide my own reactions. On the spot we generated enjoyable activities—building a school, joking about my tortilla-making, making up new games with the children.

Despite the new people who had entered my life after Dave left, I ached with loneliness. "Staying put" meant to me that I could tell others only a very little about what was going on. I felt I had no one with whom I could share the pride I was beginning to feel in how I was holding myself together, or the pleasure I took in the strides Lisa, Brett, and I had taken in our relationships. I felt there was no one to appreciate the "me" I was discovering in the turbulence. I now know I was wrong. Both Brett and Lisa saw and valued the "me," just as I was savoring the strength and goodness I saw in them.

After six months Dave returned, saying he thought he could continue to work on his issues while living with us. Although we exchanged no new promises, I once again felt chosen as a life partner. Following the old lessons, being "good" enough, had served me well, I thought. For months, however, I walked on eggshells, waiting for the structure of my life to fall apart at any moment.

Over the next three years I slowly relaxed back into the pattern of our days. Dinnertimes once more became times of laughter and sharing. The weekend outings to our lake cottage resumed. Dave and I continued to support each other in parenting and our careers, but we also engaged in marital counseling with the therapist we had grown to trust earlier and introduced new joint activities into our lives—Saturday breakfast dates at a nearby cafe and weekly Spanish classes with two couples from my church.

Our life together seemed, to me, better than ever. I kept going to church and exploring friendship. Brett rebuilt his life, working as a short-order cook and moving into his own apartment. He discovered a passion for conflict-resolution efforts through his volunteer work at a center dedicated to peace education. He became a full-time employee, and later, Executive Director. Lisa finished high school in grand style and went off to Hampshire College. On our thirtieth wedding anniversary I stood in church, during the time for spoken celebrations and concerns, to celebrate our marriage.

Within six months, however, Dave again announced without warning, discussion, or any reason I could understand that he was leaving.

"I cannot live with you, and probably not with anyone."

Once again, I was taken unaware. We were busily making plans to travel together in Brazil during our upcoming sabbatical leaves. We had just returned from a rich week of family hikes and board games in the mountains. And, a day or two earlier, I had stood beside Dave as he told others at a New Year's gathering of his joy in our time together.

I was in numbing shock and shaking uncontrollably, but I insisted that Dave talk with both Brett and Lisa before he left. We reached each of them that day, and they came individually so that he could tell them his decision and try to answer their questions. Then he walked out of my life that very evening, and I heard nothing from him for several weeks. Long stretches of time followed when I didn't know where he was staying or how to reach him quickly in an emergency, and there was almost no contact. My life had shattered completely.

Gifts

With Dave's second leaving, there was no question of my staying put, waiting, and hoping. The very foundations of my life—Dave and the old lessons—had proven untrustworthy. Finally I saw the lessons for what they were: myths of control. They couldn't keep fear at bay. There would be no life partner for me. Despite all my effort, my life had fallen apart and, I thought then, the nurturing family I so wanted for my children.

At first I spent most days weeping, walking, and just trying to get through the tasks I couldn't avoid. I went through the motions of life—washing, eating, teaching—yet feeling dead inside. The shell that was me kept showing up, at work and in church. I wouldn't let others see my downfall. Shame was trying to crush everything alive in me. But I swore to myself: For my children I will find a way to survive in this "aloneness" that has haunted me from childhood.

Strangely the sense of absolute loss and hopelessness brought new freedom. I let myself feel and express the troubling emotions more freely than ever before. It wasn't a conscious decision. It just happened. Why hide or deny them? What more did I have to lose? And when Dave made contact, I asked the tough questions. Did you ever love me? Was all our marriage a sham? Is there someone else? Why won't you fight for this family—for Brett and Lisa, if not for me? Why can't you say what you want? What have I done wrong? You aren't even giving us a chance.

I heard no answers that helped make sense of what was happening. Faced with Dave's tears, I eventually stopped asking. But neither the questions nor self-blame went away. During the wee hours of the morning, I paced the floor in their company. Sheer movement got me through the nights as well as days.

Thankfully, Lisa remained at home for two weeks before her

college term began. Her presence kept me in touch with my need to survive. And just being beside her reminded me that life still held some forms of love.

I now had two female friends, Doris and Beth, who reached out to me. I let them see something of my anguish. They sensed when I most needed adult company, inviting me into their homes or coming into mine to just sit with me. Later, they offered other unexpected acts of kindness that reduced me to tears of gratitude—by placing a simple meal in my home for me to find upon return from a work trip, offering to drive me to and from the airport, surprising me with a birthday celebration, or simply calling to ask about my day.

After about a month, I could harness enough attention to resume a bit of my research. To my surprise, I found that visiting families of very-prematurely-born infants offered a balm. Beforehand I dreaded the drain these site visits put on my very limited physical and emotional resources. But once in the home and interacting with the mother and baby, I could forget myself a bit, recapture my curiosity about and delight in each child's development, and empathize with that family's problems. The end of each visit found me exhausted, but a bit more peaceful. I let go of most other aspects of my work. My staff took care of much more than usual, and my graduate students made more decisions on their own. I just handled the baby visits, my classes, and the graduate and undergraduate student meetings that seemed critical.

I craved friendly contact each day, and most days found it—a walk or tea with Beth, a phone conversation with Doris, a working lunch with a department colleague. Over the weeks, I began to feel part of a human community larger than my children and me.

Not quite three months after Dave's leaving my parents drove to my brother's home in a town near me, to celebrate his fiftieth birthday. I joined them for the day of festivities; but as I drove home that evening, a deep sadness descended. Not a single word had been uttered about Dave's departure or what it meant for me.

Within three days I wrote a letter to Mom and Dad, explaining how hard it was to be with them without directly addressing what is going on in my life. "I am hoping we can somehow get over this reluctance to ask or talk about how I am feeling. I know that part of my unwillingness in the past to talk with you about difficult times has been my wish not to worry you. Now, however, it seems very important to be able to talk about what is going on in my life—for me. What I need right now is the freedom to be me, with all the tumult of feelings that I am."

It was a hard letter to write—and probably to receive—but it felt right to speak out of my own need, even though my words changed nothing.

Throughout the first two years after the death of my marriage, I kept being surprised by brilliant rays of light that briefly penetrated my sorrow. I began to call these rays "gifts." I had done nothing to make them happen, or deserve them. They simply appeared, often at times of deepest despair. An unexpected kindness from Doris or Beth. A bluebird resting atop a deck railing, looking at me and singing. A new wildflower blooming along my walking path. Lisa's phone calls from college and feeling her love wash over me. A drop-in visit from Brett. A poem speaking to my heart. The calls of my resident owls. Such were the earliest rays of light, and I greeted each with a surge of gratitude.

Thinking it would be helpful to remember the possibility of light in my times of greatest darkness, I made a "gift box," a wooden box into which I put a memento of each gift. I can hold and open the box when despair threatens to overwhelm me, I told myself. But I never did. Just knowing it existed was enough.

The first summer after Dave's departure Brett and I traveled with a group from my church to work at the Mam Center outside of Ostuncalco, high in the mountains of western Guatemala. It proved more of an adventure than we had reckoned on.

We took an old Greyhound bus from Guatemala City that took three men to drive. On that rainy night, as we climbed steep mountains, one sat at the wheel, steered, and honked. One hung out the door craning to see oncoming vehicles as we traversed, with but a single headlight, one after another sharp curve in the narrow road. The third also hung out the door, reaching with a rag around toward the driver's side, trying to make up for the absence of windshield wipers. All pretence of casual talk between Brett and me had ended, and I saw his white knuckles as he clenched the metal railing of the seat in front of him. I fell asleep, to be awakened only by the jolt of the bus stopping at our destination.

The bus ride alone was enough to question some of our long-held impressions of each other. I was the controlling one, setting schedules, tasks, ways of doing things. Yet here I had seen all the danger, known it was out of my control, and just fallen asleep; while he, the one who prided himself on going with the flow, had remained wedded to his tense, straining-for-control position. Similar surprising contradictions kept happening—with the unfamiliar food, the physical strain of doing construction work at an altitude of 8000 feet, the attempt to communicate via gesture or Spanish, and all the uncertainty and concern about the guerrillas taking over Ostuncalco, the army's counter attack, and the sound of artillery and mortar fire for several days.

We had actually walked into town on the market day that the guerrillas arrived. We had seen crowds gathered around speakers in the plaza but not understood the talk; and as we hiked home we passed dozens of young men walking toward town, dressed in camouflage clothing with machine guns or artillery belts slung over their shoulders. Not knowing what was going on, we took our cues from the Mam people we were among—pausing or moving in unison with them, looking down when they looked down. Once we made it safely back into the compound, our Mam hosts showed us where the young men should hide if either side came calling and taught us the secret knock they would use to signal their own presence. Brett knew I was concerned, worried about what I had gotten my pacifist son into; but he also saw my relative calmness coupled with attentiveness to cues of safety or danger around us. We worked outside whenever our Mam co-workers did, regardless of the sounds of gun fire. When they stopped to take cover; we did, too.

Brett and I hadn't taken this trip to work on our relationship, but it helped us see each other anew and explore new ways of interacting. And, upon our return, a flurry of other gifts awaited us. Doris and her husband met us at the airport. Beth had placed a bouquet of flowers in my house and a simple meal of soup and bagels. And a phone message from Lisa welcomed us home.

A few months later, I traveled to Brazil to teach week-long courses at four universities. I experienced a warmth of hospitality beyond anything I had ever known. My hosts welcomed me into their homes, treated me like family, showed me their lives from the inside, and introduced me to their friends and favorite activities. We overcame language barriers. Professionally, we sometimes communicated through translators, or by drawing pictures and acting out young children's behavior. More personally, through a broad variety of gestures and facial expressions intermixed among words of Portuguese, Spanish, and English. I felt a strong connection with each host and, upon departure, exchanged expressions of love and the hope to meet again.

Back at home other surprises awaited me. I made a new friend, Sandy, who was a single woman too, also not by design. I found we could talk about aloneness and that talking helped. She became a first model for me of what a livable life as a mature single adult might look like.

Through Sandy, I began to try yoga. I soon found myself part of the "yoga group," five women who met in Sandy's home one night a week with a teacher. At first, we seemed so different from one another. Yet, as the months passed, this unlikely mix turned into a support group that kept up with each other's lives. We started to have dinners together occasionally, and then a weekend at the beach.

Also, after a pause of some twenty-five years, I had returned to playing the flute shortly before Dave first left. After his second leaving, I found I couldn't even pick up my instrument. Playing made me too sad. Slowly, however, I began to play again. Then I discovered that our yoga teacher, Barbara, was a pianist. We clicked musically and began to make music together almost every week.

At Duke, a visiting cultural anthropologist, Harriet Whitehead, sought me out to talk about early childhood development. She had lived for several months in Papua New Guinea, among the Seltaman people who had recently settled into an agricultural way of life. Her questions and observations piqued my curiosity. Soon we were jointly planning a research project that would involve her returning to their villages deep in the jungle and, with their permission, videotaping the interactions among their young children and audio taping adults' descriptions of the children's behavior. We faced intriguing challenges. How could we drop into the jungle the large auto batteries we needed to power our equipment? How could we explain to the villagers what we wished to do and why; how could we get truly informed consent? What could we offer in return? How could we determine children's ages in a culture that didn't assign ages to their children? Would the new approach we were taking to a comparative study of infant development really work? As we talked and plotted—as ideas, questions, and possibilities whirled in my head—how good it felt to be alive with intellectual excitement.

I was discovering that life contained gifts as well as troubling emotions. Moments of light, joy, and gratitude were all intermixed with my times of despair, sorrow, and loneliness. In many gifts I experienced new forms of meaningful human connection—the new friendships, the church community, my Brazilian hosts, the yoga group, music making with Barbara, the new research collaborator, and more freedom in my interactions with students and faculty colleagues. I discovered that I was held within a web of human connection. No one thread was as thick as the one I had forged with Dave, but this new web could perhaps provide at least as much support for life as my marriage had. I was beginning to understand that the web was more "gift" than the product of my own "doing."

Other rays expanded my web even more. These were moments in which I was immersed within the beauty, the wonder, of nature and felt a deep connection to all that exists—to birds, flowers, trees, a southern swamp, the song of wind blowing through a forest. Fear of aloneness was giving way slowly to a new vision of interconnectedness.

My children offered other life-giving lessons. Brett reminded me often: "Lisa and I have grown up in a nurturing, loving family. Nothing can take that away, Mom." And I saw that Brett, Lisa, and I still were a loving family, only in a new form. As their dad began to come back into their lives, I realized that he and they might also form a supportive unit. I could not make that happen, but I could be hopeful and encouraging.

Lisa and Brett even showed me that I had something of value to offer them in my time of darkness. Brett wrote on a handmade birthday card: "It is wonderful to see you face loss with courage and openness. This is just one of the important lessons I have learned from you." Thus my children helped me stop dwelling on what I had not been able to provide them and see what I could give—and was giving them—just myself, my love, and my imperfect example.

The first Christmas alone came and went; and with Sandy's coaching on survival skills, I made it through. She helped me envision new holiday rituals. Since Brett and Lisa would be spending Christmas Eve with Dave, I arranged to have supper with friends that evening and to attend our church's "love feast" with them. Christmas morning the children and Mom and Dad were with me, and Brett and Lisa took over Dave's old role of secretively stuffing my Christmas stocking. Witnessing their delight in conspiring together was an unexpected gift of the season. I asked Bill and Shirley to host our family Christmas dinner that year so I wouldn't have to face Dave's absence from my table.

On New Year's Day, I drove to the North Carolina coast to perform a ritual. I took with me three beautiful, smooth stones. On one I wrote "the past;" on the second, "Dave;" and on the third, "fear of the future." I walked the beach for some thirty minutes, found a place in the dunes to reflect on what I was about to do, and then walked to the surf to throw away each of these pains. I chose to start with the one marked "Dave." When I gave it a mighty heave only to have it fall at my feet, I collapsed on the sand in laughter. But I quickly stood again and let "Dave" sail far over the breakers. Then I threw the other stones, at least as far.

As I retraced my steps along the beach, I felt a warm sense of peace and oneness with all around me: the sea, the sunshine, the breezes, the surf, the pelicans skimming the crests of waves, and the sandpipers racing to and fro at the surf's edge. A sense of well-being stayed with me throughout my first meal alone in a fine restaurant, and during the drive home.

The second Christmas, Mom and Dad came to visit for a week. And during their stay—two years after the complete collapse of my old life—Mom's life fell apart.

Mom's Life Shatters

Mom and Dad drove over 500 miles to spend Christmas with me. They had finally decided to visit nearby continuing care communities and to seriously consider moving to my area since I was anchored here and Bill was nearby. But shortly after they arrived, Dad fell ill at my home with what at first seemed only a bad cold. Rapidly, however, he became more ill. Two emergency room visits followed, with returns to my home and extensive caring for him there. Despite all our efforts, Dad suddenly became unresponsive. Then came an ambulance and paramedics, hospital admission, and within a day Dad was on a respirator in intensive care. We discovered that he had double pneumonia and perhaps reactivation of the TB he had had when I was four. Mom's anxiety over Dad, and her own start of a respiratory illness, exacerbated her chronic lung disease. She, too, was hospitalized (the very same day as Dad) and put on oxygen support.

The next three weeks brought several unsuccessful attempts to wean Dad from the respirator, and then finally success and his gradual improvement. Daily I wheeled Mom, oxygen tank and all, from her hospital room to the intensive care unit for visits with Dad. Eventually Mom was discharged to a nursing home to undergo further respiratory therapy. Dad moved, with a good prognosis, to a regular hospital room.

A few days later, Brett and I were celebrating his birthday with a special meal in my home, when a call came. Dad had developed massive bleeding. He was back on a respirator in intensive care. I should come at once. Mom and I needed to decide quickly whether to keep him on the respirator.

I rushed to the hospital as Brett hurried to Mom at the nursing home. I tried to reach Bill, but could only leave a message. As soon as I could arrange for a nurse at the home to monitor Mom, Dad's doctor and I began a phone conversation with her.

"Recovery seems highly unlikely at this point. We think massive damage has already occurred," the doctor explained.

Thankfully, Dad had been able to tell us his wishes before being put on the respirator the first time. "Put me on it only if there is a good chance of recovery." Still, making the decision now was difficult. But within several minutes, Mom and I decided to remove him from the respirator. The doctor urged us to have him removed right away, and we agreed.

Just as Brett reached Mom and began to make arrangements to transport her to the hospital with all the necessary oxygen support, I rushed to Dad's side. In recent days he had told me how very tired he was and discouraged. He had drawn strength then from my holding out hope that he would feel stronger in time. Entering Dad's room now, I simply embraced him and said, "It is time to rest, Dad." He looked to me from a far-off place. I think he understood my words. "It is time for you to rest now."

The breathing tube was removed as I held him. When his mouth repeatedly moved but no words came, I told him: "I will take care of Mom. There is no need for you to worry." After several waves of convulsions and doses of morphine to alleviate pain, Dad slipped away. It took perhaps no more than forty minutes, but they were long ones in which I saw and felt agony. Only at the end did I realize tears were flowing down my face and that one of Dad's doctors was holding me and crying, too.

Brett got Mom to the hospital shortly after Dad's death. Although I had been hoping she would arrive before his passing, I was thankful then that she hadn't witnessed it. The interim pastor of my church arrived just before Mom, and about an hour later, Bill and his family. We all gathered around Dad, along with the intensive care staff that had cared for him over the last four weeks, to engage in a time of prayer and remembrances.

Mom suddenly found herself without her husband, without her health, without her home of over thirty years, without the ability to ever again live independently, and without any of her friends nearby. Her old life was gone and could not be recovered.

After three weeks in the nursing home, she was able to move temporarily to an assisted living facility near me. Several months later, when Mom was well enough, we flew back for a last visit to her home on Long Island, made decisions about what to do with all her belongings, and spent time with her friends. Eventually Mom moved into the assisted living portion of a continuing care community twenty minutes from my home.

I realize now, although I did not then, that Dad's death was for Mom like Dave's leaving had been for me. She, too, had grasped onto a male to make life more livable, to feel more secure and less scared. For over sixty years, so much of her existence had been anchored around making life better for her husband. Now he was gone. Only her son and daughter and their families were nearby in this new life. Then, within a little over a year, Bill and his family moved far away. It was Mom and I, and both of us in the process of constructing new lives amidst the rubble of the old. Brett lived near enough to visit weekly; but Lisa was at a college a day's drive away.

After almost forty years apart, Mom and I were once again daily companions—the only daily companions for each other.

Unexpected Joy

Eight months after Dad's death, I made the first of a surprising string of discoveries. I was preparing for my second trip to Brazil and looking forward to being with some of the people I had felt strong connections to during my first visit. Amidst periods of deep sorrow, I was continuing to experience gifts of nature and meaningful human contact. The new friendships were deepening and nurturing me more and more. I was playing my flute with Barbara, my pianist friend; and we had even worked up the courage to invite my mother and the yoga group to a concert in Barbara's home. Then four new human connections came, one right after the other. None was particularly remarkable, just things like a chance meeting with a favorite high school teacher of my children or running into a friend at the theater and being introduced to her Brazilian companion only to discover the many Brazilian friends we had in common.

Suddenly and unexpectedly, I found the words forming in me—"Trust life." All at once, I discovered I did. Surprise, happiness, and a surge of new freedom flowed through me. It was as if a huge weight had suddenly lifted off of me. I did not understand what was happening. It all felt mysterious, but exhilarating.

My time in Brazil was full of reconnecting with old friends and making new ones. When I returned, I began reading "spiritual" books. Since Dad's death, I had become better acquainted with our interim minister. In response to my questions about Dad's dying—the convulsions and the seeming agony of it all—she directed me toward books on death and dying, through which I came to know such writers as Frederick Buechner, Thomas Merton, Kathleen Norris, and Henri Nouwen. Sandy gave me another "spiritual" book for Christmas, *Spiritual Literacy* by Frederic and Mary Ann Brussat. This contained short quotes on such topics as grace, forgiveness, and faith—words drawn from novelists, writers within different spiritual traditions, and others. As I read the section on faith, I had the sudden discovery that what I had been experiencing—gifts, trusting life, oneness with the world around me, and openness to mystery—others called "faith." This was a shock to me. I had equated faith with a set of beliefs, a creed, not with the experiences I had been having.

Shortly thereafter, and with great timidity, I explained to the interim pastor what had happened as I read and asked her, "Could I have faith?"

She laughed. "I wondered when you would discover that!"

I made another surprising discovery around the same time. When I was alone, I sometimes talked out loud. I would be sitting quietly by myself and words would just pour out—words about what was going on in my life, my feelings, my hopes, what made me so thankful, what I was working on, what I needed help with, and concerns I had for other people. Strong emotions surfaced as I talked: sadness, longing, grief. Occasionally they were times of just expressing an overwhelming sense of gratefulness.

These talks felt important. They brought a kind of peace. I had no routine for engaging in them. Suddenly I would just feel the urge to talk. Soon, I found myself daily expressing aloud the hope that I would grow in this peace and remain open to others—listening, empathizing, loving, offering what I had to offer, and accepting with gratitude what others offered me. Only months later, when I read Henri Nouwen's book on prayer, *With Open Hands*, did I come to think of these times as "prayer." I had unclenched my fists and was opening myself to I-knew-not-what, to a mystery that I later began to call "God."

Then came what felt like the most courageous move of my life.

Over the past three years, Dave had moved from almost no

contact with me to initiating near-weekly visits. He came to express his wish for us to be "very good friends" and his hope that he could continue to care for me in times of illness or emergency. I found his behavior confusing. With one hand he had pushed me away; with the other, he was drawing me to him. I was uncertain about how much contact I could handle, but, guarded, began to meet for walks or meals. I was still wrestling with a host of questions. Who was he? What of my view of our marriage was valid? Had he ever loved me? Was any kind of friendship possible for us? Our times together seemed important for finding answers. And he was the only adult who had witnessed most of my adult life. I found it hard to let go of the person who had seen me more than anyone else during those years. I told myself that if I began to feel worse after our contacts, I would stop or lessen them.

One evening Dave told me: "I'm going to go to some singles events. I don't know whether I will feel like dating or not."

The hurt and fear I felt at his announcement showed me that I had not really let loose of Dave. I was still clinging, hoping for some special relationship that would prove me lovable. Within a day or two I knew I had to let go. The only way I could think to do this was to stop all contact. I decided this on a Saturday while visiting the North Carolina mountains for the day. I lay awake all night after the decision and walked for hours in the woods as soon as daylight appeared. Amidst all the sorrow of this walk, I found a gift. A barred owl settled less than ten feet off my path, on a branch just above eye level. Motionless, we gazed into each other's eyes for at least ten minutes. A few hours later I met Dave and told him I needed to stop seeing him and why.

I wish I could say that I had bravely dived into my fears at earlier points, but I hadn't. I had tried to control them, or push them away. Upon Dave's leavings, I had had no choice but to struggle within the fears. It was as if I had been leaning over an edge looking into them with Dave holding me secure at the rim—

and then he let go! Now, I chose to dive.

All that had transpired since Dave initially left, my new trust in life and friends, and friends' examples of "gutsiness," helped give me the courage to take this step. But I felt I was diving off a high ledge of solid land into a free fall above a potentially bottomless pit. I had no certainty that I would land safely.

Over the next few days I felt as if a huge wave—an ocean breaker of troubling emotions—had caught me and I was spinning, tumbling out of control, unable to catch my footing or find anything to hold on to. Could I survive this? What would happen to Brett and Lisa? All I could do was cry "help." I spent time with close friends to whom I could tell what I had done. All they could do was be with me a bit while I went through my fall. I was facing head on, and by my own action, that old fear of being so overcome by negative emotions that I would disappear into the whirlpool's vortex and never return. Slowly the turbulence subsided, bit by bit, and I found myself still able to function. Ever so slowly I began to feel more like myself. After several weeks I knew I would somehow land safely and that my diving had been the right next step.

Once I felt sure of landing, I initiated divorce proceedings and redid legal papers to disentangle my life from Dave's. But even during this time I had to resist his periodic attempts to make contact, through letters that expressed his desire for friendship. I didn't respond; I needed more time. While walking with the interim pastor one day, I mentioned Dave's most recent note. Her expletive of anger surprised me, but it felt so good. Her outburst meant that someone else saw how difficult it was to be both pushed away and pulled closer.

After almost five months, I felt confident enough to agree to a breakfast meeting. We would discuss some matters pertaining to Brett and Lisa. I went in my most guarded mode, but found I could handle this contact. In fact, this meeting, and a few that followed, felt devoid of any real connection with Dave. At first I attributed this to my not letting myself just be me. If this was how I acted around him, I thought it would be better not to meet. So I tried to be less guarded during our next time together, and I did feel and act more like me. Slowly we returned to near-weekly contact; and in a matter of months, I began to feel a bit more connected. But I now knew that I had let go of any desire, or need, for a special relationship with him.

Then came the second summer after Dad's death and the slow realization that I was happy, that there was a new lightness to my mood. This was the summer Lisa spent with me while taking courses to prepare for graduate school.

In July I traveled to Switzerland and France. A brief meeting in Switzerland with friends of friends led to a week of living with them, at their insistence. Days, I explored their country as a tourist. Evenings, I stayed up late into the night with these new friends, discussing their lives and mine. Next, I traveled to France to speak at a convention where I expected to see few people I knew. Instead, I found that my path had crossed with several of the folks there; and we sought out chances to talk and share meals. After the conference, a research colleague asked me to join him and his parents in a day trip to Chartres. I accepted; and we entered Chartres Cathedral, fortuitously, when its labyrinth was opened to the public. We could walk this serpentine stone pathway that had been laid into the floor around 1200 AD. Accompanied by live cello music reverberating throughout the sanctuary, I walked a labyrinth for the first time, letting its eleven concentric circles lead me along a weaving, twisting course to its very center and then out again. I felt deeply connected to all who had traversed this path over the centuries, my feet fitting into the imprints their feet and knees had carved into the stones. This trip, indeed the whole summer, strongly affirmed my growing sense of human interconnection.

At summer's end I drove Lisa to Cornell and as I recounted earlier found the collage entitled "Unexpected Joy." I discovered then that I was living a whole new life—one aptly described by these words. During the seven and a half years since my old life had begun to fall apart, I had moved from despair to a life of trust, faith, and unexpected joy.

The next night, on my way home along the Skyline Drive of Virginia, I stayed in a lodge perched on the side of a mountain. Looking out the window of my room, I witnessed the most glorious sunset I had ever seen. The sky seemed to join me in shouts of joy. In the morning I hiked to an even higher point where I could look out on mountains and valleys, all around me. As I stood on a rock ledge jutting out into space, I felt like a butterfly upon release from its dark, constraining cocoon. Surges of gratitude flowed through me and a sense of freedom—of openness to all I surveyed.

Part III: Exploring Unknown Territory

Embracing Love

During the next three years I continued to integrate Mom into my life while working full-time at Duke. We shared meals together at restaurants, weekend visits in my home or hers, the house concerts Barbara and I offered, evening phone calls, and Brett and Lisa's visits. Despite the increased contact, I sensed little change in our relationship. But seismic changes were taking place elsewhere in my life. I moved more deeply into the unfolding world in ways I now realize helped shift me for the surprising journey Mom and I were about to undertake.

I ventured into this unknown territory called "faith"—without maps, any written directions, or a human guide. I don't recall feeling scared, though curious perhaps and tentative. Most salient was my longing to experience more of the loving presence that had led me here.

That desire kept me sensing my way along, step by small step. And seemingly around each curve, I found companions and wonders hitherto unknown. Occasionally I caught glimpses of how a few paces had led me to a treasure—like a new bond of human love or more silence in prayer. I would pause to write about that segment of the journey. My next steps, however, often went in an apparently different direction—perhaps to grief over my past or to finding words of others that fit my experience of the sacred. No vision of a single path emerged, nor a destination point. But with each new encounter my longing grew to know, to taste, more of this landscape.

Sitting down to write about this period several years later, I reread all I had written at the time. More accounts emerged than I remembered—eight, ranging in length from six to forty-four pages. I arranged in temporal order, from earliest to latest, all the discoveries these writings helped me recall. As I studied my list, five recurring themes leapt out: human interconnection, prayer, words for faith, the desire to serve, and forgiveness.

Could I now find more order in what at the time felt like abrupt jumps between different lines of discovery? I pulled out the large data pads of my research life to create a picture of the temporal flow. I divided the page into five columns, one for each theme. A common metric, the number of months since entry into this new territory, ran down the page. I could place almost all my list's findings within this two-dimensional space. The resulting picture was of five streams flowing side by side down the page, with multiple bursts of discoveries within each. But still I could detect no apparent order in how the action jumped back and forth among the themes. I glimpsed a few points at which the streams influenced each other, but a detailed story of how they went together remained beyond my grasp. Nevertheless, I sensed that each flow had carried me deeper into faith, perhaps toward a common destination point that I could not yet envision.

Within the stream I named "Embracing Love," I discovered an unimagined abundance of meaningful human connection. During my journey toward faith, I had let down several old protective barriers. I was more open to others now and found love offered — seemingly all around me.

The new friendships at home became stronger and richer. I began to offer "Music Together" afternoons in my home, in addition to the house concerts we had been doing at Barbara's. Barbara and I performed the piano and flute pieces we had worked on, and I invited friends to offer their music, a poem, or a story. Each year new folks joined in.

I found a mentor and friend in the new pastor of our church. A year into this new life, as I prepared for the serious operation mentioned earlier, Pastor Mark and his wife helped plan support for my children in case unforeseen complications arose. They spent time with Brett and Lisa, read the "within despair" tale I had written, and were ready to offer support should anything happen to me.

The week-long hospital stay and lengthy recovery period provided a rich opportunity to experience anew the strength of my web of human connections. Old fears surfaced briefly from time to time. Could my children provide the daily care I needed? Would the other people of my web seek out contact when I couldn't initiate the interchanges we had been having? As the weeks dragged on, surely they would tire, think of me less often, or begin to view their times with me as burdensome obligations. Did they know me well enough to guess what I would like or need?

What I experienced put the old worries to rest. Brett and Lisa were marvelous supports. And during the actual operation, when they most needed support, Dave was there for them. Then when Brett and I lived together for three weeks, our roles reversed, we managed my convalescence with good humor and even grace.

Close friends visited, listened to me, reported from the larger world, discussed "deep issues," or simply sat beside me. They brightened my room with flowers and pictures. They brought books, their favorite CD's, vegetables from the farmers' market, and stories of healing. Later they helped me climb my walkway stairs and stroll the lanes around my home. Later still, they reintroduced me to the broader world with rides around town, meals in carefully-chosen restaurants, and grocery shopping. They seemed to intuit what I needed before I knew it myself. How different this was from my past efforts to manage medical problems on my own, sometimes even hiding them from Dave.

Cards and phone calls came from my church community, work colleagues at Duke, and acquaintances near and far—even from people I had not told about the operation. Dinners arrived for Brett and me during the first week at home; later, when Brett went back to work, breakfasts and lunches. People offered Scrabble and Yahtzee games, videos to watch together, books and poems, tapes of our church services, companionship and conversation. When I began one day to list the people I wanted to thank, I quickly had a list of over forty. I realized my web stretched much farther than I had ever dreamed possible.

During these weeks, I read an essay by Henri Nouwen, "Receive All the Love that Comes to You." Nouwen writes about experiencing a pain that despite all his efforts he cannot get rid of, for it exists far deeper than he can reach. He likens it to a turbulent river flowing far down, in a frightening place within him, but asserts that one day this river will be quiet and peaceful. If we can welcome and take in all the real love that comes our way, he suggests, one day this weakest part of our self will be attracted to and let itself be immersed in that deep glow. In the weeks surrounding the operation I embraced more love than ever before—and welcomed the hope that one day my tumultuous river would become tranquil.

After my recovery, the connections forged over the past several years in other countries bore new fruit. A Brazilian colleague joined me in North Carolina for a year. She and her family gathered around my table for their first Thanksgiving and first taste of turkey. Another Brazilian friend joined us several months later. In Norway, I visited a woman who earlier had spent six months working on her dissertation with me. We sat together amidst toddlers in daycare settings, and sailed the coast of Norway. I worked long-distance with Brazilian, Norwegian, and Canadian colleagues on a cross-cultural exploration of toddlers' social worlds, fashioning a symposium that soon had us traveling to China. My anthropology colleague and I found creative ways to communicate and coordinate our research activities between Papua New Guinea and North Carolina.

Would I have been as open to exploring these new connections had I remained married to Dave or wedded to my old lessons? I doubted it.

During this same time period, a stranger and I began to connect in a way neither of us suspected possible. A year earlier I had volunteered to meet weekly with Laura, a young adult living in my community with severe mental illness. We set our sights on the goal of taking walks together through the woods near my home. Laura experienced severe paranoia. As we set out each week, her head swiveled from side to side, looking for danger. But we went just a bit farther each time. After several months, the day arrived when we made it all the way to where I customarily turned around on solitary walks. I slapped my hand firmly on the metal pole marking this point and turned around sharply, congratulating Laura. To my amazement, her body shook with laughter. And was that a tear rolling down her cheek? Until then I had witnessed only flat affect or fear. When she regained control, she smiled right into my face and exclaimed with a chuckle: "You're neurotic, too."

From that moment on, laughter as well as tears became part of our weekly meetings. And over that year and the next we came to trust each other. She, to tell me things she hadn't yet been able to talk about with anyone, and to trust me when I insisted she needed to bring this to her social worker or psychiatrist. Me, to see and delight in how she learned to keep track of me in my bouts of illness and travel, and to relish her calls to express concern for my health or pleasure at my return. I remember my surprise and sorrow when she said: "You know, you are the only person who meets with me just because you want to."

Although I began our relationship in order to give back a bit for all the support I had received during my time of despair, I quickly learned how much Laura offered me. I experienced real connection with someone whose thought and feeling patterns were so different from mine, and witnessed her courage in living each day. Together we celebrated the small steps we each took in facing our inner demons.

Early in these years I also discovered a whole new form of human connection—spiritual companionship. First I found what

I called a "spiritual guide" in Pastor Mark. As I sought to understand and deepen the spiritual dimensions of my discoveries of "trust," "faith," and "prayer," he listened to my ponderings and shared his own. He guided me to readings and helped me find connections with what others have felt and thought. Later I discovered that something called "spiritual direction" existed, and realized that Mark and I already had been engaged in an informal form of this for most of a year. We continued to meet monthly, and began to read and discuss spiritual memoirs, contemplative spiritual classics, and books on process philosophy—a passion of his. I also sought out a formal relationship with a spiritual director, Jeannene, and started meeting with her about a year into this new life of faith.

With Pastor Mark and Jeannene I could speak of my deepest longings and share my experiences of mystery and the surprises of prayer. I knew that my yearnings made contact with their own and that as we talked, we both were grounded in the mystery I called "God." The Quaker mystic, Thomas Kelly, gave me words for this new form of human connection:

> "When we are drowned in the overwhelming seas of the love of God, we find ourselves in a new and particular relation to a few of our fellows...a new kind of life-sharing has arisen of which we had only dim hints before...God is the medium, the matrix, the focus, the solvent...It is as if the boundaries of our self were enlarged, as if we were within them and as if they were within us...."

Lisa's marriage to Aaron brought new bonds of love stretching across conventional family and faith boundaries. They wanted to be married in Ithaca, amidst their Baha'i community. A month before the ceremony they welcomed my invitation to throw an engagement party that would bring together my close friends, Lisa's high school friends, and several local Baha'i families. It would be my first opportunity for extended interaction with these families that had nurtured Lisa's faith during her high school years.

My artist friend Sandy and I transformed the large room that served as our church sanctuary into a warmly festive setting for a sit-down dinner. Pastor Mark offered the blessing, and a Muslim caterer prepared the food—a man I had come to know and value during my search for a Turkish coffee pot for Lisa years earlier. People of different faiths mixed easily around the tables and talked of their faith traditions. After dinner, people stood to share warm stories about Lisa and Aaron. Barbara and I played a simple arrangement of "Simple Gifts" before launching into a much more flamboyant version.

At the wedding, I shared a room for two nights with Aaron's mom, a Baha'i teacher. We exchanged stories of our children and faith. Lisa and Aaron asked both their mother and father to escort them to the altar, a request that expressed their strong sense of family despite the parental divorce each had experienced. Brett served as Lisa's primary attendant; and Aaron's brother, as his. Upon recessing, the two mothers left together, arm in arm, followed by the two fathers, while a string quartet played their own version of "Simple Gifts"—at Lisa and Aaron's request.

Drawn Into Silence

Another stream of discoveries began with my desire to try a set-aside daily time of prayer. So far my talks with mystery had been spontaneous—words just pouring out of me when I was alone. Their unplanned appearance meant to me that they were unforced, or not solely of my own doing. They seemed evidence of some two-way connection between mystery and me. So it was with trepidation that I began planned periods. But I had been reading about "rules" of a spiritual life (*The Rule of Benedict* and *The Rule of the Society of Saint John the Evangelist*) as well as about ways of meditating in Avery Brooke's memoir, *Finding God in the World*. I wanted to try starting each day with prayer.

At first I used the daily rituals provided in Edward Hay's *Prayers for a Planetary Pilgrim*. I discovered that nothing felt forced about deliberate periods of prayer. They still had a life of their own. After reading Thelma Hall's book on *lectio divina* (*Too Deep for Words*), I wanted to try this more meditative form.

My times of *lectio divina* (sacred reading) fell into the pattern of first expressing yearning for the sacred in a few words, like "Here I am." Then I would read a short scripture passage aloud, two or three times, listening for its message to me. Often a word, phrase, or sentence would "light up." If so, I silently repeated those words, savoring them. I then would meditate on what had been given. Sometimes I visualized what was happening and put myself in the scene, imagining the dialogue and other sensory impressions. Or this portion of the passage might connect immediately with some issue in my life, like my feeling broken and unable to be healed, and I would explore that connection for the new insights, images, or nudges to action it might yield. Other times, the segment evoked a flood of strong emotion, and I simply stayed with the feelings. At some point in the meditation, however, I spontaneously broke into verbal prayer. The words at first built seamlessly upon what had arisen during meditation, but they often moved to other, recurring prayer themes. Eventually, all words ended and I remained in a silence mostly free of thoughts or named feelings. The quieting sometimes came earlier in my prayer time, or was interspersed throughout. At times I had a sensation I can only describe as "letting go" and "falling into mystery."

For over a year these times of *lectio divina* brought rich insights and a sense of close communion or dialogue with sacred mystery. But then they began to seem empty, barren. I started to use more and more words at the beginning, expressing my desire for receptiveness to whatever might be offered in the day's passage. The barrenness, however, continued.

One day I suddenly listened closely to the starting words I had been saying for several weeks: "For God alone my soul waits in silence" (Psalm 62.1) and "Be still, and know that I am God" (Psalm 46.10). On that morning I finally heard the invitation to become quieter. I let go of almost all words at the start and began to experience more interior silence throughout *lectio divina*.

I went to my first retreat, drawn by its focus on "self-emptying" and its leaders, Rose Mary Dougherty and Tilden Edwards of the Shalem Institute for Spiritual Formation. Driving to this event with some people I had just met, I learned it was to be a silent retreat. We would be in silence for roughly forty hours! If I had known, I suspect I wouldn't have wanted to go; but half way to Washington, D.C. in someone else's car, I had no choice.

Other surprises followed. The prolonged silence drew me into a more profound quieting than I had ever guessed possible. It took about twelve hours to first enter into this deep space. Then I found myself longing for even more lengthy stretches of exterior quiet, hoping to taste more of this interior stillness.

The first morning after returning home, I tried a new form of prayer. I began with some whole body movements I had experienced at the retreat. I stood and stretched my arms high above my head as a gesture of yearning, before bowing deeply to the earth to express surrender. Then I sat, conscious of only two words. As I breathed in, I thought the word "God" and as I breathed out, the word "love." The silent words continued, but in time I became less aware of them and found myself in something like the deep quiet of the retreat. This form of body and breath prayer now became my regular morning practice.

Five months later, I sat among 1200 people in a church near my home listening to Thomas Keating offer a workshop on centering prayer. I had read some of his books and had briefly tried centering prayer on my own. But at this session I came to a new sense of this practice.

Gerald May's *Will and Spirit,* about the struggle between the ego's willfulness and our desire for willingness, had connected deeply for me. As I listened to Keating, I saw centering prayer as a way to express my intent, my willingness, to surrender. I could not make this happen; but I could express my desire for what I had come to call "radical commitment," for surrendering thoughts, feelings, sensory impressions, and images of myself and God—all my attachments—to the boundless mystery of God.

Centering prayer became my way of beginning each day. My sacred word was "willing." I sat in silence, and whenever I caught myself grasping at a thought, word, image, or feeling, I would gently and silently use the word "willing" to express my intent to let it be. There was nothing magical about the word. It just drew me back to my desire for simple open presence. Spontaneous verbal prayers, *lectio divina,* breath and body prayers, and the liturgical prayers of church services continued, but centering prayer was now the staple of my prayer life.

At the end of twenty or thirty minutes of centering prayer, I continued to sit in silence. As people and concerns floated into awareness, I held each in prayer. When I began this form of intercessory prayer, I often silently said a word or two about my hope for each person or issue.

Soon I just held them, wordless.

Finding Words

Within a third stream flowing through these years, I found words that enabled me to express more of my sense of sacred mystery. Experience has been the bedrock of my search for meaning throughout life. Labels and more abstract concepts come later. The lessons drawn from my childhood were distillations from a host of everyday events. I have no memory of having any words for them before my late forties. Only then, and after the "good life" collapsed, did I examine the largely unconscious guidelines I was living by and begin to clothe them in words.

I had entered college with the vague expectation that I would become a civil rights lawyer. But in my sophomore year another door opened for me, in my first psychology course. I saw a simple form of order emerge amidst all the complexity of human behavior, in a study of how adults memorized a string of nonsense words. The professor drew a curve on the blackboard that summarized the number of errors made as a function of the word's position in the list. A smooth bell-shaped curve appeared—fewest errors for the first position, a few more for the last, and then progressively more for words closer to the middle of the list. I was dazzled. Screwing up my courage, I approached my teacher at the end of class.

"Where can I read more about that curve?" I asked.

"Here. Try this chapter," he suggested. "And if you want to, make an appointment to talk with me next week."

Our first meeting led to weekly sessions throughout the semester, a tutorial within the field called "human verbal learning." By the course's end, I had a summer job with one of his colleagues—to do my own observations of people memorizing strings of words. By graduation, I had published two research articles. I was hooked. When I began graduate studies at Columbia, which was a hotbed of research on animal learning, I hoped to integrate studies of how humans and animals learn.

My thirty-plus years of research into early development also have been decidedly experiential. At a time when others were emphasizing infants' anxiety when separated from their mothers, Harriet Rheingold and I noticed newly-crawling infants contentedly leaving their mother's side at home, in airports, in parks—with a smile even. We created research settings to learn more about how often and where they went. Virtually all ten-month-olds who could crawl or walk quickly left their mother's side to move toward a distant toy. They went to a novel toy rather than a slightly familiar one, and to a newly-opened doorway instead of one they had previously entered. Also, they chose to approach and smile at the less familiar of two new women. And when two identical toys were present, they chose to go to the one a new adult was touching even if that meant crawling over the other toy. Instead of starting with a theory and looking for behaviors to support it, we turned to abstract words or concepts—exploration, social facilitation, evolved behavior— only later, after all our hours of observing babies in action.

I used a similar experiential mode of inquiry, though I wasn't conscious of it at the time, in my journey toward faith. When faced with new mysteries, I suspect I tried to use whatever tools had worked for me in the past. The break-up of my marriage initiated a host of new happenings. Some of these I could group together on the basis of a common element—events that, say, suddenly and unexpectedly eased my despair. Repeatedly having my darkness penetrated and lightened—this order— caught and held my attention. I searched for words to describe the experience. "Rays of light" felt right. I examined the contexts in which the rays arose—often at times of deepest despair, when I was struggling just to survive. A bluebird alighting outside my window, looking in and singing to me as I sat weeping, too beaten down to even stand. I began to call the rays "gifts" in that I had done nothing to bring them about. I recalled how the "gifts" made me feel: That I could continue. That there was something good in life. That I was not alone. I embraced the words "a loving presence."

In time I connected the word "God" with this presence. As a five-year-old in Detroit, I had gone to Sunday School long enough to hear the words "God is love" or "God loves you." Around that time, I stole a lace doily from a friend's house and took it home hidden in my underpants. Clearing the floor of my closet, I smoothed out the lacey fabric and centered my Bible on it. For days, I would sit before my open closet door, gazing upon my altar. I didn't dare share with anyone the precious hope of love and acceptance that these items seemed to hold. Mom found my altar one day, dismantled it, and escorted me to my friend's home to apologize. Over fifty years later, the word "God" became a name for the mysterious loving presence I had sensed within another darkness.

Other early words—"prayer" and "faith"—arose in a different way. I couldn't use the manipulative techniques of science to test my ideas, but I read about others' spiritual journeys, finding experiences that were like mine and examining the words the writers used. Some words and phrases lit up for me, the way they had in *lectio divina*. Words that felt "just right," I adopted as my own. I embraced "prayer" as I read in Nouwen's *With Open Hands*; and "faith," from the Brussats' *Spiritual Literacy*.

By the end of the first year of my new life of faith, I had written the story of my despair transforming into unexpected joy, using just the faith words "gift," "loving presence," "God," "prayer," "trust," and "faith."

I was also reading widely within the Christian contemplative tradition: the classic writings of Teresa of Avila, Catherine of Siena, and St. John of the Cross as well as the more contemporary works of Thomas Merton, Tilden Edwards, Gerald May, and Beatrice Bruteau. I also sought out books on prayer and meditation. My in-the-flesh spiritual companions, Mark and

Jeannene, together with these book companions guided me to more and more words that fit my experiences. Slowly I became able to express more of my encounter with sacred mystery.

"I wish I hadn't been baptized as a baby or confirmed as a teen-ager," I told Pastor Mark one day, "because now I can affirm my faith in a whole new way. I wish there was some way to do this within the church, but I guess there isn't."

I think I saw a glint in Mark's eyes as he said, "I think I can arrange something."

Within a week he handed me copies of two church rituals. But I knew I couldn't say their prescribed words wholeheartedly. When I expressed my misgivings, Mark threw me a challenge:

"Write your own statement of faith."

"Oh, I don't think I could do that," I said. But I put the possibility in the back of my mind, hoping some inspiration would come. It came, when I least expected it.

I was in my favorite diner waiting for Dave to join me for a breakfast meeting. As the moments passed, I thought I could use the time to jot down a few thoughts about what might go into a statement of faith. I begged a piece of paper from my waitress and began. To my surprise, words kept coming. Dave never showed; he had forgotten. But I stayed and before I knew it, I had a draft.

I read the statement to Jeannene, and then Mark. "Have I captured in words what you know of my journey?" I asked. "Am I saying anything 'heretical'? I would at least like to know if I am."

They reassured me on both points.

But Mark added, "Now plan out all you want in the service and write your vows."

If he had mentioned these tasks at the start, I doubt I would have found the courage to proceed. But within a few weeks I knew what I longed for: silence, musical offerings interspersed among short readings, and the opportunity to express in my own words my faith and vows. The vows came easily once I realized they were the words that repeatedly formed in me during prayer to express how I longed to live in relationship to sacred mystery and all of creation. For the readings, I chose short passages from writings that had resonated with me and given me words. Some addressed experiential awareness of the sacred; others, trust and the desire to open more fully to the sacred.

I asked three of my musician friends from church to participate. A pianist would offer a prelude that set a meditative tone and later accompany me in a joyous rendition of "Amazing Grace." A guitarist would compose and sing a piece about trust and praise; and a harmonica player, offer "Joyful, Joyful We Adore Thee." I hoped everyone would join in the Taize chant, "The Lord is my Song."

"A Service of Coming to Faith: A Celebration" came into being, not quite two years after the discovery of my new life. Mark and Jeannene conducted the service. Brett and Lisa came and more than thirty others I had invited, including one of my Duke research collaborators, a man of Jewish faith with whom I had shared faith discussions. I regret now that I did not invite Mom. She had shown no interest in church for several years, and I did not want to risk sharing with her what had become so important to me.

"I believe in God," I told the group, "in a mystery beyond all human understanding that is the source, or ground, of all creation.

"I believe that love and goodness and trustworthiness are central features of God—that life can be trusted, that nothing can separate me from the love of God.

"I believe that part of the essence of God is manifested in every aspect of creation and that we are created in God's image. God, however, is more than all of creation; God exists both in and apart from creation."

To explain how I had come to these "beliefs," I shared two quotes about sensing God. The first came from the theologian Abraham Heschel's book, *God in Search of Man*:

"The certainty of the realness of God does not come about as a corollary of logical premises, as a leap from the realm of logic to the realm of ontology, from an assumption to a fact. It is, on the contrary, a transition from an immediate apprehension to a thought, from a preconceptual awareness to a definite assurance, from being overwhelmed by the presence of God to an awareness of God's existence."

The second I found in one of Philip Newell's books on Celtic Christianity, *The Book of Creation*. He speaks similarly, but uses more everyday words and a metaphor from the nineteenth century Celtic teacher, Alexander Scott:

"Our knowledge of God…is an experience of God that comes to us in the use of our inner senses, whether that be through the scriptures and sacraments or through creation and one another. It is not a doctrinal or propositional knowledge, says Scott, but belongs 'to some deeper part of the human being.' It is like the way an infant comes to know its mother:

"'What do its senses reveal? Forms, colours, motions, sounds; these are not a soul, but through these it detects the presence of a soul, answering to its soul…Even thus does a knowledge of the Highest Spirit come through the universe.'"

For me, "faith" had become an experience of and openness to a mystery that penetrates and binds together all of creation, and whose love and trustworthiness I respond to with answering love and trust. I use the word "God" as a name for all of this. If sometimes I speak as if God were a person, it is not because I have this image of God, but because this is the language in which I can best express my sense of relationship and communication with mystery.

Putting into words what I wanted to say about my journey felt important to me, and the hugs and tears after this unconventional ceremony affirmed my sense of community. A visiting minister friend told me: "I wish everyone could claim their faith in this way."

Later I spoke to a Presbyterian student group at Duke on the topic, "A Scientist Thinking about Religious Experience." I found I had words here, too. I shared my journey as a scientist and a spiritual pilgrim, explaining why I felt no conflict between my research life and my embrace of faith. A lively discussion followed when I read physicist Chet Raymo's image of all our scientific knowledge as an island in a sea of mystery, and comparative religion scholar Huston Smith's distinction between "scienticism" and science and his reminder that surely the processes science discovers may be part of the way God acts in our world.

I also began to discover what I call "emergent words"—words that simply appear without any searching or reading. Earlier the words "Trust life" had sprung up in me, seemingly out of nowhere, giving me a taste of this possibility. But now a three-day silent retreat at the North Carolina coast led to a new awareness of the relationship between wordless silence and words.

I would go to a quiet spot in the ocean dunes or to the salt marsh and silently savor all that I sensed visually, aurally, tactilely, or by odor or motion. For long stretches of time I felt acutely present to and somehow merged with all the sensory input. At some point, however, I would become aware that a single word—perhaps "kin"—or a phrase—"just as I am"—was silently repeating in me. These words seemed to emerge out of the wordless silence; and once they entered my consciousness, they enriched all the sensory impressions. When I left my place of silence, I would feel a strong urge to return to my room to write down the word or phrase. I discovered that putting just a single word on paper often unleashed a stream of further words—words expressing thoughts, impressions, longings that I had not been aware of until that very moment.

I seemed to have let go of the control of my own words.

Sensing a Call

I also began to feel a strong desire to offer others something from my new life. After recovering from my operation I sought out opportunities to talk with people who might open my eyes to possibilities: ministers, clinical social workers, a pastoral counselor, a hospital chaplain, and leaders of Stephen Ministry programs. All I knew was that I felt drawn to service that somehow integrated spiritual issues with human needs. It was in these conversations that I first heard the words "spiritual direction," from two people who suggested I might want to talk with Jeannene. Her way of responding to my blundering question—"What is this thing 'spiritual direction'?"—had led me to start meeting with her as my spiritual director.

By the end of our first year of meeting, several experiences converged to make me wonder whether I was being led to become a spiritual director myself. I knew first-hand the fruits of receiving spiritual direction, how helpful this form of spiritual companionship could be. I had found strong experiential connections with the writings of Gerald May and Tilden Edwards and longed to move more deeply into the contemplative path they wrote about. Both men were centrally involved in the Shalem Institute for Spiritual Formation and were mentors for those sensing a call to offer spiritual direction. Perhaps most telling, a few of my acquaintances sought me out to talk about spiritual issues.

At first I fought the idea of becoming a spiritual director. Wasn't I way too young in my life of faith? But both Mark and Jeannene encouraged me. For most of a year I held this possible call in my heart and prayers. Then, in the months following the "coming to faith" service, a cascade of events affirmed the rightness of pursuing this possibility.

I met with the head of student religious life on Duke's

campus, to learn about ongoing activities I might become involved in. Our lively, intense discussions of faith and science led him to suggest that he refer a student or two to me for "spiritual mentoring" if the opportunity arose.

Jeannene, who had been listening to my ponderings and misgivings for months, asked: "Would you like me to give your name to two people I know who are seeking spiritual companionship?"

"Yes," I answered, but only after quizzing her about why they wouldn't be better served meeting with her.

Something in me also said "yes" to another of Jeannene's suggestions: "Why don't you just try writing the application for the Shalem spiritual guidance program? See what happens as you write. You don't need to know at the start whether you will actually apply."

When I sat down to begin, I found that words just poured from me—evidence of where my passion lay. I gave the draft to Jeannene and Mark. "Would you be willing to recommend me?" Both said "Yes."

For the first time I formally offered spiritual direction to someone, one of the women Jeannene had sent to me. My only "training" was my own faith journey and the meetings with Jeannene and Mark. Nevertheless I felt grounded, relaxed, open, and deeply attentive. Words just came.

I met with a Roman Catholic chaplain on campus, Sister Joanna, and found three of my hopes answered within this one meeting. When I asked about ongoing student activities, she suggested we offer weekly meetings where students could join us in a group form of *lectio divina*. After hearing of my interest in the Shalem program, she described the group of spiritual directors she met with—the Wild Geese. "Would you be interested in becoming a member?" she asked. Participation in such a group was a requirement of the Shalem program. Overwhelmed by what had already transpired, I didn't mention my third wish—for her to supervise me. But a few minutes later, she asked: "Would you like me to offer you supervision?"

The very next day, Jeannene sent me a copy of her recommendation letter. It showed me how well she knew my limitations, as well as strengths, and yet how strongly she supported this direction for me and why.

I sent in my application, with no hesitation. And a few months later I received notice of my acceptance.

With great joy and clarity, I entered the two-year program.

Wheat and Weeds

I also began to love and forgive myself. The first movement within this stream of discoveries came in response to one of Jeannene's questions: "Despite feeling your love neither received nor reciprocated by your parents, why did you remain a person who could love?" Pondering her question led to revelations that transformed my previous ways of thinking about my earlier life. I had never thought of God as being any part of this earlier story. But some neglected memories emerged and revealed my blindness.

The first to arise were of the times with my maternal grandfather mentioned earlier, his walks and talks with me during my teenage years. Only now did I realize that his presence in my life was a "gift" that had helped keep love alive in me.

Then a new connection arose between Grandpa's death and the birth of my first child. I had long grieved not being able to visit Grandpa as he was dying. After three miscarriages and an operation that might enable a live birth, I was pregnant with Brett.

"You must choose between this child and visiting your grandfather," my gynecologist advised. "Any travel at this point places the baby's life at risk."

I chose to not gamble, but continued to grieve over not seeing Grandpa, and that he had not lived to know Brett. We had all been through a very difficult period with the suicide of my cousin. I wanted the awareness and joy of a new birth for Grandpa—his first great grandchild.

Suddenly, a different connection between Grandpa's death and Brett's birth arose—a joyous link. As my grandfather who had helped keep love alive in me died, my son was born whom I could love and who would teach me to love more fully. I began to sense the existence of a loving presence throughout my life.

Discoveries like these, together with all I had come to know about my old myths of control, plunged me into grief. So much support for my life had been available, but I hadn't even acknowledged it. Instead I had erected barrier after barrier, trying to control life and keep fear at bay.

Into the midst of this grief came the first residency of my Shalem program. On a Sabbath morning mid-way through the gathering, I set out on a long walk through the rural countryside. Wheat fields bordered my path. From a distance, they looked marvelously uniform and full of life-sustaining plants. As I approached one field, I looked more closely. I even stepped deep into it to see more. What caught my eye were all the "weeds," all the forms of life that could hinder wheat's growth. Some were quite beautiful to behold; I remember one with especially appealing purple blossoms. Others looked ugly to my eye.

As I studied the field, I saw my life as a mixture of life-giving wheat and many weeds. I recalled, too, the parable of the wheat and tares in Matthew's gospel. I began to think in a new way about the wounds of my life, my old lessons, and how long it took me to recognize the loving presence I call "God."

God had planted the life-giving wheat in me, and in all of creation, I thought. "An enemy" — human separation from God — had planted the weeds, or tares. Weeds had sprung up in my life through others' brokenness, and my own. I am this mixture of wheat and tares, and will be throughout life, for the weeds and wheat have grown together and are inextricably intertwined. The weeds remain part of my story. I cannot rip them out. But I can choose to no longer nurture them. I can feed instead the life-giving wheat.

Later that day, I gazed from atop a rise onto this now distant wheat field. The wind blew, continuously, bending the individual wheat stalks to create beautiful patterns across the field — an image of Spirit flowing though all of creation. I thought of myself as one tiny patch within this large field. From such a vantage point I could not see the overall pattern but I could sense and participate in the movement, and rest in trust. The weeds I've discovered, and will continue to discover, do not have any all-powerful hold on me. All of them together have not been able to snuff out, or unalterably damage, the life-giving wheat that is my core.

As I lay sleepless late one night, words emerged in me: "I have kept inviolate my image in you. I have kept inviolate your soul." I cried long and hard, realizing for the first just how damaged I had been feeling, how broken and unable to be healed. And that so much of my life had been a waste. But now I knew that although weeds may have grown over and obscured my wheat, they had not violated my essence. Embracing this promise started me on a path toward more love and forgiveness of myself.

Barely a month later I traveled to Iona in Scotland, to mark my sixtieth birthday. I joined the local community at morning and evening services in Iona Abbey, a stone Benedictine Abbey from the 1100s. Despite the Abbey's soaring ceilings and stained glass windows, there is an earthiness to the space symbolized by the ferns growing out of its stone walls and some simple windows that look out over grazing lands and the sea. I loved these services that framed my wanderings amidst the natural beauty of this island, and delighted in the unexpected opportunity to play my flute from the alcove high in the stone wall beside the altar.

My last evening on Iona, I went to the weekly Healing Service. The gospel reading that evening was the story of the woman taken in adultery and brought before Jesus for stoning. Jesus suggests that he who is without sin throw the first stone, and one by one the would-be-stoners slip away. Alone with the woman, Jesus says that he does not condemn her either. He forgives her and tells her to go and sin no more.

After a few moments of silence, a woman seated across from the liturgist offered an imaginative narrative of the woman's story, from the woman's perspective. She had given herself to a man who promised to marry her, but he had died at sea two days later. When it became known that she was pregnant, she refused to give the father's name in order to spare the family from disgrace. She bore twins that looked quite unlike one another, spawning stories of two fathers and of her being a whore. She had not had sex again until today when she had been swept away in love. The men had interrupted this brief moment of joy and dragged her through the streets to stone her. Then she met this gentle stranger, Jesus. His words saved her. He seemed to look deep into her, to know her entire story; and he forgave her—enabling her to forgive herself.

I was drawn into the woman's story, identifying with her and her experience of Jesus. All at once I knew I would approach and kneel on the floor in the laying-on-of-hands portion of the service. I did so as a way of honoring my new awareness that I am forgiven my life story, and am asked to forgive myself. If sacred mystery can know and forgive me, surely I can forgive. The weight of guilt and grief lifted, freeing me to live the new life of faith more fully.

Barely two months later, the new journey with Mom began in earnest. By this time, four and a half years after Dad's death and six and a half years after the end of my marriage, I had let go of many aspects of the old lessons. I trusted life, trusted God, and trusted the loving presence within me and others. I was letting go of leaning on others—whether male partner, friends, or children—to fill the void of aloneness. Increasingly, I was leaning into God and sensing the deep interconnectedness of all creation. I longed to move even more deeply into relationship with sacred mystery and to serve others from that place of grounding.

But I had not yet let go of my old relationship with Mom or my habit of "doing." Through all the old lessons runs one theme—act, do, problem-solve. It's up to you. I embarked upon the new journey still holding this old baggage.

Part IV: A New Journey with Mom

Breaking Old Patterns

Mom and I had continued to interact mostly as we had all my adult life. But a few glimpses of newness had emerged.

Shortly after Dad's death, Mom said to me, "I love you." It was the first time I remember ever hearing these words from her. She thanked me, too, for being with Dad as he died. I held close these new expressions; but I assumed they spoke mostly of Mom's heightened vulnerability, her greater need of me, and her regret about not being present at Dad's death.

Mom also began to pay more attention to me. Dad's absence seemed to free her to attend more to others, and now especially to me. Although she looked at and talked to me more often, I did not sense she saw anything of the inner me. I thought she just needed my "doing" more.

We also observed each other in new contexts. Mom watched how I interacted with other folks at her assisted living home. She could see I responded more freely with them than I did with her, and she saw some of these interactions develop into friendships. When I shared meals with Mom and her new acquaintances, our table filled the dining room with lively talk and laughter.

I watched Mom reach out to help others in her new home. At the dining table, she leaned close when talking to the woman who was hard of hearing and offered to cut the meat for the man with limited vision and tremulous hands. I saw her desire to please her fellow residents and caregivers and her courage in actively building a new life for herself. She spent little time bemoaning her fate; rather she moved quickly to find new ways to structure her days—joining in group activities, seeking out folks to talk with, and arranging and rearranging her belongings. I also noticed her pleasure in my visits.

One ritual that had evolved after Dad's death was an evening phone call to Mom on the days I hadn't visited. For over four years, the pattern of these phone conversations was much as our talks had been throughout my adult life. But it was during one of these calls—at age eighty-seven for Mom and sixty for me—that our first big step toward a new way of interacting emerged.

In the old pattern Mom recounted all the incidents of her day and then perhaps asked about mine. I assumed she was doing so out of politeness and routine, not out of real interest. I would give a brief summary, something like: "Oh, this was one of my big teaching days. It was quite busy but good." Mom then would quickly return to telling more details of her day.

On this particular evening, as Mom recounted her day's events, she was expressing displeasure at almost everything; and I was feeling the old need to calm her and make things all right. It went something like this:

Mom: "I went to music class this morning, but Mr. X wasn't there. I didn't like the new person."

Me: "I'm sorry he wasn't there since I know you like his classes."

Mom: "Two women sitting by me got upset about the noise my oxygen makes. That clicking. I can't go there anymore."

Me: "That would be a shame, Mom, because I know how much you usually enjoy the class. I bet Nurse Ella could turn the oxygen tank to continuous flow. It wouldn't click then during the class. Will you ask her, or do you want me to talk with Ella?"

In the midst of our conversation, I felt the old pain. I wanted to be seen and cared about, too.

Mom: "They took so long serving lunch and..."

Me: "Well, my day was fun. I don't often go to the Farmer's Market early on Saturdays, but I did today. A friend and I went together. The market was great, very festive. Beautiful flowers and vegetables galore. And we kept running into people we knew."

To my surprise, Mom listened and began to ask questions that sounded like real interest. "Whom did you meet?" "What did you buy?"

"I met Jim and Doris. You remember them, don't you? And I bought fresh green beans and some home-grown tomatoes. Also I got some goat cheese that's made on a farm just outside of town...."

In a while, Mom returned to recounting more of her day. But now she presented events as interesting stories, rather than troubles to complain about.

"My friend, Marge, came by this afternoon to tell me about her grandson's visit. You know, she really enjoys his visits."

This was our most pleasurable conversation ever. I had let down some of my defenses and spoken out of my desire to be seen and heard—I even interrupted! I had challenged my old assumptions about Mom and been surprised.

I began to experiment during subsequent visits and calls. I soon realized that by changing my responses, I not only avoided prolonging painful interactions, but I also freed Mom to be a different self from the one I had known. She sounded less fearful, less self-centered, and less judgmental. We both were breaking out of old patterns.

Letting Go of Resentment

A medical crisis precipitated our next big step. Any respiratory illness was potentially life threatening for Mom, given her chronic obstructive pulmonary disease. Unfortunately she developed pneumonia. During the long hours in the emergency room Mom became increasingly fearful and more intensely self-absorbed. Over the past several years, I had noticed this intensification with each of her illnesses, and I had become aware of my own reactions. I was experiencing the full force of Mom's fear and self-focus at the same time that both she and I were looking to me to take care of her. These times highlighted poignantly the experiences of my youth and reactivated my old feelings of sorrow and longing. Now, as an adult, I thought I understood the old reactions and that I was dealing with them well. So when they surfaced again during this illness, stronger than before, I was perplexed.

One day, during a meeting at church, I noticed a book on a table beside me—Henri Nouwen's *The Return of the Prodigal Son*. I had enjoyed many of his books and had not read this one, so I asked to borrow it. At first there were no surprises. Like Nouwen, I could identify with the prodigal son and feel great thankfulness for the father who forgave him. This part of the story paralleled my discoveries of a loving presence and of being forgiven.

But then I began to puzzle, with Nouwen, about the other major figure in Rembrandt's painting—the older, dutiful son who stands erect and at a distance, looking without joy at his father embracing the younger son. Nouwen articulates so well the older son's likely resentfulness. How he would reproach the father in thought and words for not loving him specially. He had been dutiful and responsible for all those years, at great cost to himself. Surely he was the one who deserved to be loved. Yet here was his father throwing a feast for his brother, something his father had never done for him.

I suddenly saw so clearly that I, the dutiful daughter, had held on to resentment of my mother for what I saw as her preference for my brother. Old scenes flooded in: Mom buying new pants and shirts for Bill and washing and ironing them, while I wore clothes from Grandma's church rummage sales that I laundered and pressed myself; Grandma's Sunday fried chicken meals, and how I craved to, at least once, taste a piece of breast or liver. But first choice always went to Dad and Bill, and then Grandma and Mom.

Seeing my anger—naming it—helped me let it go. Sorrow over loss remained, but the bitterness and unwillingness to forgive slipped away. In their place arose a spacious new freedom in being with Mom, even in this time of her intense self-centeredness and my long hours of caregiving.

Later, aided by both Nouwen's writing and Jeannene, I became able to begin to identify with the father, the one who could forgive and love and give of himself unconditionally. I knew that I had taken on the role of being mother to my own mother from early in childhood, in part out of my own neediness and as an attempt to minimize the events and feelings I found so difficult. But for most of sixty years, I had held on to resentment as I mothered Mom. Now, I was in the old role but in a whole new way—just as a loving, caring person trying to be with another in need.

For some time, too, I had been aware of my difficulty in verbally expressing love for Mom. Even choosing a Mother's Day card was a long, tortuous process. Since Dad's death I had sensed Mom's desire for me to respond to her new expressions of love, but I had only been able to say, "Thank you." A few months after her recovery from pneumonia, Mom faced the second medical crisis of the year, an operation to repair a broken hip. The procedure was risky, given her severe lung disease and the need for general anesthesia. As she was being wheeled into the operating room, I found myself saying, quite naturally and unselfconsciously, "I love you, Mom."

Journeying into Dementia

Other powerful lessons followed upon Mom's third medical crisis of the year. It began as only a respiratory illness that could be handled in her community's health center. From the start, however, Mom's fear about this illness far exceeded everyone else's. As soon as I entered her room she would declare: "This is it!" I sensed the strength of her fear, but I was unable to soothe her. She didn't seem to even hear my questions—"What are you worrying about, Mom?"—or my reassurances.

The next day she seemed even more distraught. She talked, mostly to herself, in a rambling, hard-to-understand way about death and how people simply went to the health center and died. She was preoccupied with fear of dying.

Her distress elicited my old need to calm her and make everything all right. I left, feeling a failure but determined to get advice from others. That evening I talked with a social worker who had worked for years with the elderly. I called a friend who had cared for her mother during her long months of dying from cancer, and I talked with Pastor Mark. In all the conversations one phrase stood out—"simply be a calm and caring presence."

"Simply be a calm and caring presence; simply be a calm and caring presence." The words flowed out of me like a mantra as I drove to visit Mom the next day. When I entered her room, Mom began at once to talk about dying. This time I listened calmly, with all my attention, letting go of any concern about what I should do or say. Occasionally I nodded in understanding, placed my hand on hers, or offered a sentence that reflected her thoughts. After twenty minutes or more, Mom stopped, gave me her full attention, and simply said, "Thank you." It was the most intimate conversation we had ever had. And Mom's simple "thank you" felt like the most genuine expression of appreciation I had ever received from her.

Driving home, I shouted out with joy, "This is easy!" For most of sixty years I had tried to be a calming, caring presence and thought I was doing a good job. But this time felt so different. Without my own neediness in play, I had been able to give myself to Mom more freely and lovingly, the way I do when I'm offering spiritual direction. I had listened closely from a place of simple open presence. I was emotionally engaged, yet detached. I wasn't trying to control what happened.

Shortly thereafter, the words "simply being" began to ring within me. I didn't know why, or where they came from. Perhaps they were triggered by the mantra "simply be a calm and caring presence." At the time, I only sensed that they were pointing toward some new way of living—toward something I was approaching step by slow step during this journey with Mom.

But there was little time to rest and ponder. Mom's illness worsened quickly. Pneumonia developed again. Her heart rate increased alarmingly, and a serious irregularity of the heart rhythm appeared. We again were in the emergency room throughout a long night, and then in cardiac intensive care for several days. This was a time of relative calm before the onset of a tempest.

The storm began when Mom recovered enough physically to be moved to a regular hospital room. At first I thought her mental confusion, lack of memory, and fear were understandable, given the extreme demands that had been placed on Mom physically, the unfamiliarity of her surroundings, all the confusion within the hospital, and all her new medications. So I was somewhat alarmed when Mom began to talk about being abandoned in a railroad station and called me throughout the night, begging me to rescue her—and later when she talked about our both being on a boat in a violent storm. But I held out hope that these fears would abate once Mom recovered more and returned to familiar surroundings.

At first Mom seemed calmer back in her community health

center. Soon, however, the tempest flared again and in an even more disturbing way. Stories about the railroad station and the violent storm returned, but now Mom began to claim that she was dead. We all were carrying on a huge charade in pretending she was alive. She became angry and belligerent, shouting at me: "You're a liar!" She expressed great fear about all those caring for her. She recounted again and again bizarre, fearful stories about her caregivers' roles and their power in "this place." She became greatly attached to a male aide, calling him her husband and protector. She called for him repeatedly and tried to interfere when he cared for others.

For several weeks, these periods of paranoia and disordered thinking were intermixed with spells of lucidity when Mom seemed quite like her former self. Again, the old reaction: "I need to fix this for Mom." I brought in a psychiatric social worker. Together we tracked the episodes of disordered thinking and mapped them onto changes in medications. We worked with the doctors and nurses to get her off those that might cause mental confusion. Brett and I introduced a "reminder board" that told Mom and her caregivers when we had last visited and when we would come again, in an attempt to help Mom know, when she became frightened, that she was not alone.

Surely it was up to me to initiate and guide this problem solving. After all, no one at the health center knew Mom as I did. No one else could detect the marked changes in her thought patterns as easily as I. Seeing how exhausted and emotionally depleted I was, Brett tried to pick up some of the load. Thus he, too, experienced the storm. We both had heard Mom talk for years about her fear of "going crazy" like her mother. Her worst fear seemed about to be realized. Brett, too, began to look to me to "fix it." Nightly discussions began about what I might do the next day, as well as conversations about his feelings in all of this.

I can describe these weeks only with the word "hell." I was emotionally and physically exhausted. I lived each moment knowing that I could not perform responsibly all that I needed to—all that I felt necessary for Mom, for Brett and Lisa, for work, and for my training in and offering of spiritual direction. Each day Mom seemed to slip further and further away from us, from her old self, and from her life of lucidity. I felt helpless as I watched her disappear and inadequate in helping Brett deal with his alarm over the changes. Fresh waves of anger at my former husband washed over me. Dave had left me so alone in these parenting roles. I seldom felt God's presence in the moment-by-moment struggles of each day. I felt very alone. In a distant way, I was aware of the presence and caring of friends; but there was no time to be with them. And how could they help me with Mom?

Into this "hell" came the monthly supervision meeting with Joanna. All I could talk about was all my difficult feelings and my exhaustion. After listening for quite a while, she suggested the phrase "experiencing crucifixion." I doubt I ever would have used these words on my own—for either Mom or me—yet something in them resonated with me and affirmed the invitation I was just beginning to hear.

"Let go of problem solving, Carol, and your sense of responsibility for your mother. Trust more radically in all of this."

Over the next few weeks both Brett and I began to accept that we could not fix Mom's confusion, which became more and more pervasive. There were no more changes in medication to try. Her dementia was not fixable.

We began to feel our way toward how to be with her in all she was experiencing, sharing our discoveries with one another. I again found my way toward calmly and attentively listening to Mom. When I listened in a caring way, without any attempt to dispute or redirect her thinking, I often sensed her fear and could address it. Occasionally I could connect something in the present with what I knew about her past and join her in a bout of reminiscing, about both happy and sorrowful times.

I realized a further gift in my friendship with Laura. During our five years of weekly meetings, she often expressed her anger at others and her fears, at length and in ways that made no sense to me. But I had learned how to be a calm presence in the face of her turmoil and to love her just as she was. Our relationship aided me now in finding my way with Mom.

The calmer I became, the more Mom shared her confusion with me. It was painful to hear her self-awareness and her fear. I could not begin to imagine how Mom felt, losing her memory and thinking. Yet I sensed Mom found some comfort in talking about her confusion, in having it confirmed and accepted by me.

As I let go of attempts to control and entered more into just being a calm and caring presence with Mom, I became increasingly aware of a loving presence accompanying us. I had lost to dementia much of the mother I had known all my life, and I felt the loss keenly. But I knew that neither Mom nor I was alone in this journey.

In Dementia

Dementia began to teach me—and I think Mom, too—about the fruits of being present in the moment. Amidst the pain, confusion, and losses, we found times of beautiful, life-affirming interaction. A great example is what happened when I mentioned that my birthday was approaching. Mom's immediate response was concern.

"What can I do to celebrate it?"

"How about choosing a birthday card for me from all those cards you keep in your desk," I suggested.

Mom liked this idea, and we looked through the thirty or more Hallmark-like cards she had bought over the years and saved so she would be prepared. We tried to remember the circumstances appropriate for each and choose just the right card for me. When Mom had narrowed the choices down to three or four, she read their messages over and over, out loud, explaining what she liked or disliked about each one. Together we decided on the right card.

"Do you think I can write on it?" Mom asked.

"Let's see," I said, although she hadn't attempted to write in months. I got out some scrap paper and a pen and set her up at a table.

After several minutes of effort, she remarked with exasperation, "Nobody can read my writing."

I looked over her shoulder and started to read. "Happy Birthday to my..." When I hesitated over a word, she quickly voiced it. Together we read the message she wanted to send me.

"Happy Birthday to my wonderful daughter. I love you."

"That's right," Mom exclaimed.

I gave her the card she had chosen and she copied, slowly, her message onto it. When she handed the card to me and I was able to read the message back to her, she was delighted. We picked out an envelope, a racy, pink one, and she sealed the card up.

"Now don't open it until your birthday," she commanded as she handed me the envelope.

We both laughed. "Don't worry," I said. "I won't."

On another visit, Mom recounted again and again her attempts to find help for her parents and husband. They were stranded without gas in a hot car in some barren place. She became more agitated with each telling. I listened carefully. I had no knowledge of such an event, but I heard her desire to help, her helplessness, and her concern that she had been responsible for their deaths. Without contradicting her, I told her the story of how first her father had died, then many years later her mother, and most recently her husband. She listened avidly and at the end expressed great relief. "I was afraid I let them die." We talked then about how each had lived a long and full life, how she was living a long life, and that I likely would too.

Another time I found Mom listening to a singer during the Friday "happy hour." When I entered the room to join her, she looked simultaneously shocked and overjoyed. She grabbed my hand and expressed over and over how she could not have hoped for anything better than to see me. We held hands and listened to the music for a while, but then Mom became eager to leave. When we returned to her room, words tumbled out.

"It has been years since I have seen you. I am so happy to see you. I am feeling so alone. Everyone has left me because I am being so stinky."

This time I did contradict her. I reminded her gently that she was not remembering many things. "I have been visiting you regularly, Mom; and Brett, too, has come to see you each week. We are going to keep coming, even if you can't remember our visits. There isn't anything you can do that will stop us. You're just stuck with us."

I went on to describe in detail a recent happy time we'd had together, when Brett and I took her out for a special dinner on

Mother's Day. I told where we went, what she wore, what we ate, some of what we said.... Mom began first to nod her head in agreement and then to add an appropriate detail: "I had cake." She then expressed great relief in not being alone and the hope that she would remember some of our visits or that I could help her recall them.

This last visit forced me to face the reality that Mom could not hold on to, at least not in the way we do, good moments of interaction or the caring attentions of others. At first I felt dismay that each of my visits simply fell into a void, that they could not help her in any sustained way. Quickly, however, I recalled how I had sensed a loving presence within my despair. I became confident that love could penetrate Mom's darkness too, in ways unknown to me. I trusted that our times together left some imprint on her and helped her to live more calmly and confidently in what we call "dementia."

During many of my visits, Mom recounted stories that seemed to ask only to be shared, and for a conversational response or two. A few themes kept recurring. When Mom told me matter-of-factly that a black man had spent the night in bed with her, I was speechless. What was a daughter to say? I suspect my face froze in surprise for a moment, and that I rapidly moved to change the topic. By the third telling I had my wits together enough to reply, "How could you both fit in such a small bed?"

Mom looked first at her twin bed with a puzzled expression and then turned to me with a smile and a twinkle in her eye. "I don't know. He must have brought in his own bed."

We enjoyed a good laugh.

A more frequent theme concerned the arrival of a "party boat." It docked in the night and unloaded its passengers, people arriving for a party. I could respond to this topic more easily and just share Mom's pleasure in recounting the story.

"Did you have a good time, Mom?"

"Oh, yes," was the usual reply, leading to an exchange of

smiles. "But it was pretty noisy," she said, grimacing. We shook our heads, acknowledging our mutual discomfort with loud noise.

I imagined these recurrent themes, and others, were Mom's way of making meaning out of the events in her home. The male aides who appeared at her bedside to check on her throughout the night might have led to her idea that a black man was sleeping with her—and the comings and goings surrounding the ten to eleven p.m. shift change, to the party boat's arrival.

During this period, interactions with Mom were potent lessons for me, and I hope and trust for her, too. I didn't know what to expect each time I walked into her presence. So I tried to open all my senses to the nuances of her being—to her words, her looks, her feelings. Often I had no idea what she was talking about. I was unable to connect it to anything I knew about her. But I listened for, and increasingly heard, the feelings she expressed in her stories, and helped her to hear and acknowledge them too. I also felt my way toward helping her find beauty and joy in the here-and-now. "Look at the new bloom on your plant, Mom." "Oh, the cat's trying to reach the bird cage again. He's already on the windowsill." Or, we might remark on her reflection in the mirror, freshly painted finger-nails, the taste of a bite of food, a story shared.

Our interactions helped me see what was immediately present and find the blessings in it. I could not plan, organize, or otherwise control our time together. I had to be fully attentive and feel my way along in this awareness. Each time with Mom invited me to remain grounded in the moment, to be fully "there" with another, and to savor the gifts.

Mom, too, was experiencing new freedom. Dementia had broken her shell of defenses wide open. She no longer tried to hide or deny her fears, anxieties, or anger. She expressed them, if not in words, in tones of voice or facial and bodily expressions. And she did not shy away when I engaged her around these troubling emotions. Also, she now initiated conversations she had studiously avoided before.

A striking example was her not remembering that Dave had left me. She now frequently asked about Dave, and expressed surprise each time I reminded her of our divorce. But the conversation did not end there.

"Was the divorce your idea?" "Is it hard for you?" "What did you do?" "How does it feel to be alone?" "Is there another woman?" "Are you happy now?"

When Dave left, Mom had been unable to ask any of these questions. She couldn't even express sorrow about his leaving, or sorrow for me. Nor had Mom been able to listen. If I expressed anger or pain, she told me I shouldn't feel that way—or, at least, that I should refuse to acknowledge these emotions. What a different mother I was experiencing now, one who was able to accept her feelings and attend to mine.

The events of another visit spoke eloquently of the changes in Mom. I found her engaged in a bingo game with several residents. I joined them, as I had on earlier occasions, appreciating Mom's ability to still manage this game and aiding her and others when they became confused.

I then accompanied her to the Friday "happy hour." We sat at a table with a woman Mom knew from her assisted living days; and when another, newer acquaintance entered the room, I beckoned her to join us. I found myself seated between Mom and this new acquaintance, Alice.

With the piano music and the singing of old tunes, it was difficult to talk at the table; but Alice leaned over to me at one point and asked, "How is your mother doing?"

"I think pretty well," I replied. Then I turned to Mom and told her what Alice had asked and what I had said.

Mom smiled at Alice.

A few minutes later Mom had a message for me to convey to Alice. And we proceeded through a few exchanges in this way.

I noticed that the other woman at our table had made silent, tentative clapping movements at the end of songs. When the next song drew to a close, I looked toward her, smiled, and clapped in unison with her. Together we made a sound that started a chorus of clapping throughout the room. We exchanged broad smiles and more applause after the next song.

Mom grabbed my hand, leaned close to me, and said: "You are a very kind person. You make people around you happy. I have noticed this." She looked directly at me and smiled as she said this.

I smiled and said, "Thank you."

This was the first time in my life that I can remember feeling really seen by my mother. She could express herself directly, and I could openly receive her appreciation. What an abundance of grace.

New Grieving

For months I had been thinking about the decisions that might lie ahead, about whether and how to pursue aggressive medical care as Mom's lung disease progressed. I hoped that, when we faced the next medical crisis, the lessons of the recent past would help me let go of my tendency to grab for control.

Mom became lethargic and began to experience great difficulty in breathing. Within a week, despite regular medical attention, Mom's condition was grave. One evening her doctor said: "I think we should send her to the Emergency Room. Her labored breathing is taking quite a toll. I don't know how long she can maintain this."

"What can they do there that can't be done here?" I asked.

He mentioned blood tests, higher concentrations of oxygen, perhaps the respirator. As I listened closely to his words and watched his facial expressions, I was also fully aware of Mom's presence beside me, the scenes from Mom's last hospital stay that were playing out within me, the lack of tension in my body, the nurse taking Mom's vital signs. Mom was as peaceful as I had ever seen her—and I was, too. Somehow I knew which decision to make.

"I want her to stay at the health center where she is comfortable and surrounded by people who know and love her. Let's treat her as aggressively as possible here."

I did not feel torn in this decision, or in doubt. The path felt clear.

I went home late that evening, made calls to distant family members, alerted my pastor, and slept a few hours. Early the next morning I found at Mom's bedside her doctor, a physician's assistant, the charge nurse and Pastor Mark. We were amazed that Mom was breathing more easily. Over the next few weeks she slowly improved. We rejoiced that she likely would survive, though at a markedly reduced level of functioning. But she kept on improving, and within seven more weeks she was close to where she had been before the crisis.

Mixed in with my awe and wonder about all that had happened, I had a recurring thought. This unexpected gift of time with Mom must be meant for something, I kept saying to myself. I had no idea what this all meant, but I sensed that I needed to remain open and see what arose.

For about a month I experienced brief, intense periods of sorrow. I would be driving and my chest would begin to ache. Tears would well up and sometimes stream down my face, obscuring my vision and forcing me to pull off the road. Or I would find myself correcting a student's paper through a flood of tears. I didn't understand what was happening. Hearing of another's suffering sometimes triggered the ache and tears. Most often, though, there was nothing I could identify as the source.

One day, as I was driving home after offering spiritual direction to a woman struggling with long-delayed grief, the puzzling deep ache and tears appeared again. This time words came: "I am grieving my own loss of being mothered, my mother's loss of being mothered, and her mother's loss of being mothered." The words felt just right; and they unleashed even deeper bouts of sorrow. I knew I needed to remain with this grief—to feel it, taste it, picture it, even try to welcome it.

Over the next several weeks I stayed with the mothering-loss words whenever they appeared. I found myself remembering stories about Mom's youth. About her mother's "nervous break-downs" and how she had taken to her bed for months at a time. How at other times her mother was full of energy, sometimes even extreme in her actions. I suddenly recalled the story I had heard Mom tell, just once, about Grandma's birth and how she had lost her family. I replayed, too, scenes I had witnessed between Mom and Grandma, of Mom being criticized and berated for shortcomings. Then scenes from my youth: a ten-year-old me trying to care for everyone during Mom's backaches, a five-year-old waiting alone and fearfully outside a church, an even younger child lying alone, frightened, and restrained in a darkened room.

After several weeks, I tried to express my understanding of the grieving and its fruits in the form of a letter.

Dear Mom,

I am grieving my loss of being mothered. Intense bouts of sorrow keep punctuating a time in my life that is mostly marked by joy, peace, and greater happiness than I have ever known. I do not know if you ever experienced this grief, and if so, what form it took for you. But it feels like I am grieving not only my own loss, but yours too, and your mother's. Also, this grief seems to have opened me wider to experiencing sorrow for a variety of life's sufferings—for a family in the path of a tornado, a friend facing the possibility of her son going to war, a young mother with lymphoma, a mentor with congestive heart failure.

I need to stay with this grief, not shy away from it or attempt to deny it. I imagine myself as grieving with God—that God somehow sits beside me on my mourning bench. I sense that only by fully opening to this pain can I come to a place of rest with my loss—and, strange as it sounds, maybe in my grieving I can also release your grief and Grandma's. At times it feels like I am crying: "Have mercy on us for all the ways we harm one another and perpetuate these hurts." At other times, I gaze upon a vision of Jesus holding me and crying with me, accepting and loving me even with all the sorrow. Maybe in time I will gaze upon a vision of Jesus wiping away the tears and find that they have indeed been wiped away.

It feels like I am accepting and welcoming a part of myself long ignored or even denied. This is a wound that remains very much a part of me—despite all the steps I have taken these past ten years in trusting life and the mystery I call "God." Perhaps I am able to feel the pain now and stay with it because of these new steps—because I now trust life even when deep sorrow punctuates it. The grief does not distance or separate me from God. Perhaps it even brings me closer; perhaps I am experiencing a little bit of God's grief for us and for all of creation. Perhaps I am sitting beside God on the mourning bench, as God sits beside me.

Relating my grief to what I imagine is yours and Grandma's, too, helps me no longer distance myself from you. We are together in this wound of missed mothering. Your mother was absent from you for long periods of time, and even when she was present she was often harsh and critical. I remember, too, the story of how Grandma's mother died giving birth to her and how her father and brothers left for California shortly after her birth and never returned for her. How bereft she must have felt—of mothering, fathering, and loving family. When we visited with you during Grandma's final years, as you cared for her in your home, I remember her calling out again and again for her father and brothers—calling each of their names long into the night. It was such a plaintive sound, so full of longing. It echoes now with my grief. I cannot blame you for my loss, just as you cannot blame your mother, nor she hers. Rather, feeling now the strength of this grief and imagining that this sorrow is yours, too, connects me with you more deeply.

I do not know how it came about that I was able to mother my own children, albeit I am sure with many shortcomings. But I have mothered them. I know that with every fiber of my being. I am so grateful. I hope you can be, too—that you can feel comfort and joy that the cycle of non-mothering within our family has stopped.

I am grateful, too, for these almost six years with you since Dad's death. His death has led you to attend more to others, and especially to me. When you were first able to say the words "I love you," you made me so happy. During these past six years, too, as I have been more often with you, I have found much to admire—your reaching out to others living with you who need help, your strength in fashioning a new life without husband or old friends, your sense of humor, and your concern for your children, grandchildren and great-grandchild.

During this past year there has been much pain as your memory and thinking have changed, but these shifts also have brought with them some welcome surprises. You have let go of old defenses. You are able to face your fears, talk about them with me, and accept them. You are more peaceful than I have ever known you, more ready to simply face whatever comes. And you continue to try to please those around you and share your humor. Especially important for me has been your ability to attend to me, to express pleasure in and appreciation for me, and to see more of who I am.

Another gift of this time is my witnessing that fear does not have the last word. I have felt your terror throughout my life and seen how you have clung to others in it. I do not know your fears as you know them, of course, but I have come to imagine that they are like mine. I suspect you have felt the dread of being all alone, overwhelmed with emotions, and having no one to share them with, to ease them. I know these anxieties well. But now, I have the privilege of accompanying you near the end of your life. I suspect you are alone in many of the ways you feared—without Dad, without your son, without intimate friends, without familiar surroundings of your choice. Even with all these losses, however, I see that you are surrounded by love—divine love, the love of your daily caregivers, my love, that of my children, and the love of faraway family members and old friends. I see the pleasure you take in the "small things" or "small moments" of life. I see that you are calmer, more peaceful, than I have ever known you before. I see that fear has lost its grip on you. Fear does not have the last word.

I love you, Mom. I hope you can feel my love every time I am with you. I pray that in every moment you feel God's love around and within you. God and I are with you as you take each remaining step of your life's journey.

This letter, signed "With love, Carol," could never be read by or to Mom. She would not have understood it. But I gave the letter to her in another way. All that went into its writing changed me, and I freely gave this new me to her.

The grieving contained other gifts. I was able to embrace a long-pushed-aside part of me. Opening to the sorrow as it arose in the moment greatly diminished its power. I experienced the safety of feeling difficult emotions while also being held within loving presence. I could now embrace grief as a valued part of me, one that helped me understand and empathize with others. I saw our wounds as holding the potential for opening us so that God's love could flow into and through us, making music—like breath flowing through the holes in a flute.

I also looked more closely at my fears. As a child, I often experienced terror in the present moment: Dad's rage, finding myself alone in frightening places, feeling unloved. But now, I seldom feel fear. Most of my fearful thoughts are just that— dwellings on possibilities for the future. As I have become more grounded in the present, dread has become a less frequent visitor. And when we meet, I am more able to just stay with the bodily sensations, without trying to change them. Fear, I realized, had become a mere acquaintance—no longer something to be avoided at all costs.

I sensed, too, that something in my grieving released Mom, letting her simply be with her sorrow and fear and find their power diminished. I did not know how this could be, nor did I need to understand. I did know that strong emotional connections with my mother flowered. I discovered how alike we were in our wounds, our sorrows, and our fears. Empathy and love flowed in new measure.

Holding it All

Shortly after the season of grieving, I became immersed in a burst of new family difficulties. Within the span of a week, Mom's condition was again grave, Lisa and Aaron were facing testicular cancer, and I was living with the possibility of nerve sheath tumors being responsible for my severe leg pain. All of this, too, occurred at a time of great concern and sorrow over the impending war with Iraq.

The medical crisis for Mom developed rapidly. I was called to her side early one morning and had a few hours with her before she lapsed into unresponsiveness. She failed to respond to our talk or touch throughout the day, and her doctor and I discussed once again what level of medical care to pursue. Mom had been remarkably peaceful with me during our early morning hours, and again I decided not to seek the intensive care of the hospital. We would again treat her as vigorously as possible at the health center but this time give her medications intravenously since now she could not take them orally.

Brett joined me in the evening, and we settled in to spend the night with Mom. She remained unresponsive until four a.m., when she suddenly called out in a strong voice.

"Who's there?"

Startled, I tried to reassure her. "It's Brett and me, Mom. We are staying with you tonight. Go back to sleep if you can. We will be here."

During her long hours of unresponsiveness, I had felt deep acceptance of her death. Perhaps I even embraced it, sensing that Mom's and my journey together was at a point of wholeness and feeling some relief that her physical and emotional pain might end. But at Mom's awakening, I felt pure joy. Delight in life, even giddiness, arose amidst acceptance of her dying.

For the remainder of the night, Mom alternated between

dozing and demanding to know: "What's happening?" I stayed by her side, holding her hand, and gently trying to prevent her from pulling out her IV.

The nurses and aides who regularly cared for Mom had come into her room the day before to say good-bye to us as they left their shifts. As light broke, they now began to reappear, entering her room before starting their work. It was my good fortune to see each of their faces as they realized that Mom was still alive, and now responsive. They entered quietly, looking first toward me. Seeing my smile, they went at once to Mom's bedside to grasp her hand. They looked into her face, smiled broadly when her eyes flickered open, and greeted her: "Well, hello there." These simple actions spoke volumes about their caring.

Slowly, very slowly, Mom regained a little strength. For several weeks, however, she did no more than occasionally open her eyes for a brief moment, eat a few bites of food with our help, and doze in her chair or bed. I visited daily.

One day, after talking to her for at least ten minutes while her eyes remained closed, I said: "Well, I'm afraid I've been pestering you with all my talking."

Mom had said barely a word, but she surprised me now. "Pester on," she exclaimed with her eyes still closed.

I offered a lively monologue for several more minutes before saying, "I think that's enough pestering for today."

"Never, never enough!" was her reply.

I knew then, that even in her mostly unresponsive state, something of my love was being received and welcomed.

Now came the decision of whether to leave Mom for a few days in order to be with Lisa and Aaron as he underwent surgery for testicular cancer. The earlier removal of the testis had shown that he had a fairly aggressive form of cancer. The new surgery was to remove the lymph nodes up-stream to test for possible spread of the disease. I decided Mom was stable enough for me to try to leave.

But my severe leg pain posed a problem. For months I had been having more and more difficulty walking, for reasons that so far had defied diagnosis. Now, even leaning on a cane, I could walk only a few short distances in a day—just enough to get me back and forth to Mom. Anything more would require a wheelchair. Thankfully, Dave offered to help me make the trip. We both wanted to be with Lisa and Aaron at this time; but, if need be, Dave could put me on a plane to return to Mom while he stayed to accompany our children. During Mom's latest crisis, I had postponed two key medical exams about my leg pain. Unfortunately they were rescheduled for what turned out to be the day before Aaron's operation.

But it all worked. In the morning Dave and I spent four hours at one hospital for my tests and then took off directly to drive the six hours to another hospital for Aaron's operation. Twenty-one lymph nodes were successfully removed. Lisa, Dave and I all were able to be with Aaron during the hospital stay, and his return home. Several days later we learned that all the lymph nodes were clear except for one that showed some microscopic cancer cells.

Into the midst of all these difficulties came an event that launched me into a new awareness. It was during one of my daily visits with Mom just before Aaron's second operation. I was sitting across from Mom, talking to her and feeling a deep surge of love for her, when I became aware of the intense sadness I was feeling at the same time. This was sorrow for all my daughter and her husband were facing and sorrow, too, for not being able to share with Mom either their struggles or my own pain and possibility of tumors. As I stayed with this mixture of strong feelings, new waves of sadness and anger about the likely war with Iraq flowed through me. But then, joy arose as I saw the sky in the window behind Mom change from dark clouds to sunshine—a brightness that lit up all the beauty of early spring. I discovered I held all these feelings at the same time—and perhaps others that I was not yet aware of—and it was all right. All of this existed in the moment and I could hold it all.

As this latest burst of difficulties began to resolve, I reread words I had written earlier about the fear I had touched in grieving loss of mothering. "I have discovered that my current fears are really just fearful thoughts—about the possibility of finding myself alone, with diminished abilities, and unable to cope with overwhelming things. I long for the grace of staying in the moment, letting go of this focus on possible frightening events, and trusting that sacred mystery will provide enough if and when I experience fear in the moment."

I suddenly realized that I had just gone through a time of several hard, potentially overwhelming events. But I had experienced neither fear nor aloneness. Instead, I had sensed a loving presence with me and known an abundance of human care and help—from Brett and Lisa, Dave, the hospice and health center staffs, friends, and spiritual companions. God had indeed provided "enough." And, I had trusted and remained more in the moment than ever before.

At Sister Joanna's suggestion I tried my hand at composing a Psalm about this desire to hold all that is in the moment.

A Psalm of Spring 2003

In the shadow of your wings, I sing
for joy, for sorrow, grief, and pain,
for beauty, for each new sign of life,
for fear, for wonder, and for awe.
I desire, dear God, to sing to you for all that is—
for all each moment holds.

But how, O God, can this frail vessel
contain it all?
How can I ache with the sorrow of illness and war
and yet know joy?

How can I embrace life fully as I accompany the dying?
How can I sing a song of praise
while crying, "Lord, have mercy?"
How can my heart leap with joy at each of spring's birthings,
and fear with those awaiting new blasts of destruction.
How can I experience the deep silence of life
as I listen for the birds, the wind, the cries of despair?

I do not know, nor need I,
for you, dear One, contain my all.
You enable me to simply be once more
with all the present moment holds
each time I stumble and fall.

In the shadow of your wings,
I sing my song.

Radiance

The next few months were relatively calm. Mom recovered from her latest medical crisis and became surprisingly energetic. She began to walk again with her walker; and we resumed our weekly lunches "out," at the club center immediately adjacent to the health center. Life for Lisa and Aaron returned to something approaching "normal." He was recovering well from his operation, and they were at peace with their decision to pursue a surveillance mode of treatment (blood work, lung X-rays, and CT scans every three months). We ruled out nerve sheath tumors for me, and physical therapy was bringing the first relief from pain in a year and the hope I would walk normally again. My decision to let go of most of my hoped-for professional accomplishments during this year of sabbatical leave was sitting well with me and enabling me to devote my energies to caring for all those in my life, and me.

The calm ended abruptly. Another medical crisis emerged—a huge hematoma on Mom's leg burst open with extensive bleeding. Despite the stress of three emergency room visits in quick succession, and the considerable pain of twice daily bandage changes, Mom remained peaceful and accepting. We thought a life-threatening infection might develop, since her severe lung disease and steroid medications made healing difficult. Yet the wound slowly healed.

But there was little time to celebrate, as Mom suddenly became jaundiced. Blood work ruled out various forms of hepatitis; yet the jaundice progressed. I had to make another decision. The bile duct probably was blocked. Should we do an operation that might be able to clear it, if cancer were not the problem? Her physician felt she had some chance of surviving the procedure. Yet, would she? And if she did, how would she respond to a troubling event she could not understand, its pain, and all the drastic changes occasioned by a hospitalization? A two-hour discussion with her doctor, the hospice nurse, and her social worker led to my decision against the surgery. This choice was of quite a different order than my earlier ones. It meant her jaundice would only worsen. Her condition likely would become grave in the near future. I felt the weight of what I had done, but the words "do no harm" kept ringing in me.

When I visited Mom later that day, she mentioned how much more tired she was feeling and looked questioningly at me.

"The tiredness comes, Mom, from your body fighting an illness of your liver. We do not know how to treat it. There is one possible operation, but it's not clear whether it can help and whether we should do it. It is a hard decision."

She looked directly at me and calmly said, "Yes, that is a hard decision," before closing her eyes.

I let a moment or two of silence go by before asking, "Do you have any thoughts about what we should do?"

There was no answer.

During the days that followed, I most often responded to Mom's expressions of fatigue with just an empathic "I know." It seemed a comfort to Mom that we both could acknowledge how tired she felt. One day, however, the setting seemed right for me to ask her:

"When you feel so tired, Mom, do you think about dying?"

She opened her eyes, looked into my face with a smile, and said: "No. Maybe I should, but no."

After a pause I said, "It's so good, Mom, to just be in the present moment, savoring all that is enjoyable in it."

She listened, her face again lighting up with a smile, before she closed her eyes.

I visited daily as Mom's abdomen became increasingly distended and her skin yellowed, as she became progressively more lethargic and her periods of alertness shortened. She remained calm, responsive, and without much pain. She roused when we interacted with her. She usually greeted us with a smile. She listened to stories of my day and news from her son and grandchildren, making brief, caring comments and saying, "Tell me more." She took pleasure in our short forays by wheelchair. We might visit the caged birds, or slip out to the gardens to see the fall colors and feel and smell fresh air. She delighted in notes and cards from Lisa and distant friends, and asked me to read them again and again. She held and smiled at each new picture of her great granddaughter—Bill's son's daughter. Most of the time she knew me, although occasionally she confused me with her sister. Eventually she began to call me "Mom," usually when I was combing her hair.

I often stayed after she fell asleep to gaze upon her stillness. There was a new softness to her face despite its many wrinkles. All facial tension had eased and her no longer curly white hair hung limply around her face, blurring the boundary between head and pillow. Her skin seemed increasingly transparent despite its yellow tint. Always petite and trim, she now looked even tinier and less distinct—almost as if the physical body I had known as my mother was melting away. Only the rhythmic moves of her chest and the occasional fluttering of her eyelids spoke of life. But when she awakened, the clarity of her blue eyes and her smile utterly transformed her appearance. A center of aliveness blazed out from amidst all that was becoming increasingly characterless.

It was during these months that Mom and I threw a party. Pizza, one of her favorite foods, was never served at the health center. So we brought in a festive meal of cheese pizza, fresh pineapple, ice tea and cookies. Brett and his girlfriend Ellie came, and the staff happily joined in. They set up a table for us in a special room, complete with tablecloth, flowers, and candles. We all chatted, smiled and laughed, and enjoyed both food and companionship. Mom stayed awake and alert during the entire party, for almost two hours. When I wheeled her back to her room and kissed her goodbye, we both said: "What a fun party!" I added to myself: We have celebrated life and love, in the face of pain and death.

Throughout this time I became increasingly aware of Mom's beauty—her radiance. I saw in a new way what I had been witnessing for some time—her accepting manner, her reaching out with humor and caring to others, and her enjoyment of the moment. Piano music. A new bloom on the plant beside her bed. My companionship. A joke shared. Pizza. The pictures her favorite aides brought of their children.

Perhaps her inner beauty became even more evident to me as her body deteriorated and her activity, her "doing," subsided. It was as if all else had been stripped away and I was catching glimpses of Mom's true self. This beauty—this radiance—had been her essence all along. But it had been covered over, or hidden, for so many years by Mom's own many layers of defense, and by mine.

Dying

Aspects of Mom's radiance became harder to see. Her calm courage continued to shine forth, even in the face of increasing discomfort and the progressive loss of prior pleasures. But she less and less often opened her eyes, responded to us, or talked. She turned inward, perhaps harnessing her resources for this final period and turning her sight toward another form of existence.

I was uncertain about what Mom understood. Did she realize she was dying? Shortly before her death, we had our one and only real conversation about dying.

I arrived that day to find Mom noticeably weaker. But she greeted me with a smile, and we talked a bit. She listened for about twenty minutes, providing a brief response or two, before closing her eyes and withdrawing. I stayed another forty minutes, but during this time there were only brief moments of any contact between us. Her nurse arrived to start a breathing treatment, and I got ready to leave for the day. After kisses, hugs, and expressions of love, I left her room and stopped several feet down the hallway to talk with her nurse.

"Carol!"

I heard and rushed back to Mom's room. She had removed the mask used in her breathing treatment and was looking at me wide eyed and saying, "I want to talk with you."

I pulled up a chair beside her. "Is there something you want to talk about?"

"No."

In a bit I commented on how weak and tired she seemed today. She nodded "yes," and I found myself gently saying: "You are moving toward dying, Mom. We do not know how to make your liver problem better. I wish we did, but we just don't know how to."

She looked at me steadily as I spoke and then continued to hold my gaze for another minute or two.

I broke the silence. "Do you feel fearful about dying?"

"No, I don't think I do."

"You seem deeply peaceful, Mom."

A few moments later I added, "You have led a long and full life."

"Yes, it has been a good life—many good things," she said, easing back into her chair and closing her eyes.

I waited several minutes before saying, "I think that we all come from God and return to God."

There was no immediate response.

An aide interrupted us, and I asked for a few more minutes alone with Mom. "I am so happy, Mom, to have had these past three years with you. We have spent a lot of time together. We have come to know and appreciate each other so much more. I am thankful for that."

Mom looked at me with a smile. "I'm thankful too."

Mom's face then furrowed in pain as she struggled to change how she was sitting. I called for her aide and together we moved her into a more comfortable position.

I kissed her goodbye, saying, "I love you."

"I love you a lot," she replied.

I left saying, "I will see you in the morning."

Driving off I realized my uncertainty about leaving her just then. She seemed to especially want company, and I wondered about the impact of our talk about dying. I stopped beside the road for a few minutes of silent prayer. By the time I pulled back onto the highway I knew I wanted to return to her just as soon as I could arrange for someone to take over my evening obligations.

I entered her room two hours later. Mom became alert at once, looking toward me with eyebrows raised in surprise. "I think you want some company tonight, Mom. I got someone else to take over the meeting I was supposed to lead."

She reached out her hand to me—a rare move.

I grasped and held it.

"Thank you," she said.

Mom then talked more than usual—about her food, she had had enough and I should eat it because I must be hungry, and about the plant beside her bed that kept blooming. How many blooms were there now and is that a new one?

I drew her attention to the picture of her house that hung on her wall, and she asked: "How long have I been away?"

I told her the story of her leaving, of how she had lived there for thirty-three years, of good memories from my visits there, of who was living in her house now, of what her long-time neighbor had written to her recently.

At the end Mom said, "What a good memory you have!"

Soon she began grimacing and struggling; and before I could ask for an aide, her nurse appeared. The nurse helped Mom onto the toilet, and said: "I'm going to get M. who is your favorite. Isn't that so?"

Mom worked to reposition herself so that she could look out the bathroom's doorway toward where I was sitting. "My daughter is my favorite," she said, looking directly into my face.

A few minutes later M. and I helped Mom into bed, and she quickly withdrew into sleep. I remained beside her for about twenty minutes, replaying all that had transpired between us that day. I launched a heart-felt prayer of gratitude, and wrote a few lines to help me remember this part of our journey. Together, we had taken a big step toward simply being with dying.

I think another step for Mom came soon after. Bill, who lived on the opposite side of the country, was coming to visit. He and his family had sent Mom several letters, family pictures, and an audio tape telling her of their love; but he had not seen her in many months.

I told Mom, "Bill's coming."

Her face lit up. "I must prepare for his visit," she declared.

I had arranged with Mom's nurse when Bill would arrive and what Mom wanted to wear, but nothing prepared me for how I found her that morning. She had cooperated beautifully with her aides when they washed and dressed her and in other preparations that she had let go of months before—curling her hair and applying make-up. She sat quite upright and alert and greeted Bill with warm pleasure. She talked more, and with more animation and clarity, than she had in several weeks.

I stayed in the background as they visited. Slowly I realized that Mom was looking toward me quite often during their conversation. It felt like she was sharing with me her enjoyment, and drawing strength from my presence. She sensed, I think, my pleasure in all that was happening. Only as I look back on this scene now, do I recall my earlier reflections on the prodigal son's return. How different this time was from my "dutiful daughter" days.

In the afternoon I left Bill and Mom together, sensing his need for time alone with her. Then after a brief visit with Mom the next morning, Bill departed.

I entered Mom's room a few hours later and found a very different woman. That afternoon and evening, and for at least the following week, Mom was extremely tired and weak. She stayed in bed and barely responded to any of us.

I do not know, of course, what transpired within Mom around this time with Bill. But I suspect that being able to engage in familiar patterns of interaction with him, exchange expressions of love, and hear that all was well with him and his family enabled Mom to let go of Bill, and more deeply be with her dying.

As Mom became progressively weaker, she needed more help eating. I offered to feed her when I was there at a mealtime. The first few times went smoothly. But as she became even frailer and, I suspect, felt more vulnerable, she became impatient and unhappy with my efforts. I watched her regular aides feed, clean, and reposition her and saw her ease with them. It suddenly dawned on me that her aides, and the predictable structure they provided in these daily tasks, were extremely important to Mom. Even when I closely mimicked how they did them, it was not the same. She did not have with me, as she did with them, the long history of repeated success in accomplishing these tasks. I could not provide Mom the same security and comfort in these activities.

Wow! My surprise at this revelation helped me realize that I unconsciously had assumed that I was the primary human source of comfort for Mom at this time. Once aware of my assumption, I was able to let it go and more fully feel my way along. I stopped trying to give the help her aides regularly provided, continuing only with the daily task of combing her hair.

The discovery of this one script led me to examine whether I had other assumptions about her dying. These assumptions, these scripts, after all were a form of trying to seize control. I quickly realized another one—my need to be with her as she died. I had been expressing that desire (my need) to the nursing staff for almost three years, asking them time and again to be sure to contact me if her condition worsened. But I knew that Mom's journey had defied all predictions. When the liver problem was diagnosed, death was thought to be one or two months away. But here we were almost five months later. It was not within my power, or any human's, to ensure that I was present at the moment of her death. I let go of this need, this idea of what should be, and trusted that I would be led moment by moment. My role was to listen attentively and to respond, not to write the script.

Only then did I realize the pressure I had placed on the nursing staff. Implicitly I had communicated that it would be their mistake if I were not present at Mom's dying. So just a month before her death, I talked with each of her nurses to share my new insight and to apologize. None of us could control whether I would be present or not, and that was all right.

In her final month, Mom remained mostly calm and at ease. She seemed further and further removed from the world of living that I knew. I saw very few signs in her of pleasure in that world. At times her eyes opened and looked toward me or something else, but seemingly without seeing anything of this world. She held my hand and occasionally squeezed it as I talked to her. I just trusted that something important was going on within her. It felt right to be with her in whatever was happening.

Then one day I received a call at work from the hospice nurse. Mom had started to experience severe pain, something we had been expecting for months. I returned to Mom's side as we began to give her morphine to allay the pain. I stayed with her that day and the next, going home both nights to sleep.

On the third day, Pastor Mark and I sat together beside Mom in silent prayer. Brett came to sit and say his goodbyes. During these three days at least fourteen people who had helped care for Mom also came by to just be with us for a few moments, and I suspect to honor the passage she was about to make. Barely a month earlier, Lisa and Aaron had visited and been able to say their farewells.

I stayed with her that night, holding her hand. About three a.m., while I was asleep beside her, she slipped away into some new form of existence. No one was consciously with Mom at the moment of her death, but I suspect she felt our love surrounding her.

Part V: Surprised by Peace

No Tears

The depth of peacefulness I felt right after Mom's death took me by surprise. I was filled with a quiet joy, a greater sense of freedom than ever before, and the assurance that all was well and that all would be well.

I returned alone to my home in the predawn hours, surprised that I wasn't grieving. But I did not question my serenity. I let it envelop me. I craved solitude—time to savor the wonder and grace of our journey, the healing and wholeness of it, and this new level of peace. I felt Mom had trustingly stepped from her earthly life into some new form of being and that I had freely and lovingly let her go.

The ice storm that came that evening and closed down our town for several days conspired with my desire to be alone with all these feelings—and with mystery and awe. I felt held in a soft cocoon of solitude. I told only immediate family members about Mom's death and close friends who knew something of our story. These few people provided graced opportunities to share a bit about Mom's final hours, and their loving support surrounded me within the seclusion I craved. I floated in a sea of tranquility, feeling embraced and nurtured. I never imagined that anyone could experience such peace with the loss of a loved one and coming face to face with one's own mortality.

When I later wrote about this sense of peace, of all being well, scene after scene of a young child being mothered played out before me. I found myself saying the words "like a weaned child with its mother; my soul within me is like a weaned child" (Psalm 131.2). Have I not now experienced mothering, I thought—God's gentle presence and loving care of us? And have I not been able to mother my own mother during these final years of her life and feel her answering love? Was I resting now in God's and Mom's mothering of me?

Once our town thawed after the storm, Pastor Mark and I held a service to celebrate Mom's life and honor all those who had taken care of her. It took place at the health center with most of her regular caregivers present. Brett joined me, along with a few close friends. It was a simple service that expressed our Christian faith and yet felt welcoming and, I hoped, accessible to all. Pastor Mark's words expressed so well what he knew from me, and what he had witnessed directly, about the care Mom had received and my thankfulness for all those present. Music flowed from my flute to express what was in my heart. "Amazing Grace" communicated, better than any words I had, the depth of my gratefulness for these last three years with Mom and for all those who had accompanied us.

The service, the hugs before and afterwards, and this manner of parting from the health center community that had embraced us brought further closure to this part of Mom's and my journey. I listened to this community's sharing of their appreciation for Mom—her graciousness, her spirit, and her courage—and realized I was delighted with the person they knew as my mother. They too had seen her radiance.

Acceptance

Within a week or two I became aware that I was also at peace with my own history. I now accepted—in a new way—my entire life story. No longer was there any sense of myself as a "survivor" or a "victim" or any other label that separated me from, or pitted me against, the particulars of my life. It was just my story, my human journey; and it was all right. Gone was my longing for a different path, or blaming myself for this one. I was free of the "should-haves"—about knowing that I could not control my life or anyone else's, about making a better choice about whom to marry, about being a better wife. I was left only with what is, and with immense gratitude for my life.

I recalled an article about our absolute poverty that suggests we may need to first experience "enough" in order to freely embrace that poverty. Had I now embraced poverty—our inability to control or possess anything, including our own life story—in the aftermath of having experienced "enough" in the grace of the past three years?

"...I am no longer very good at telling the difference between good things and bad things." These words of Gerald May from *The Dark Night of the Soul* kept returning to me. They acknowledge our poverty of knowledge and express a profound trust in, an acceptance of, our life stories. May wrote about living with congestive heart failure and awaiting a heart transplant, not knowing whether these circumstances were "good" or "bad." When cancer had emerged in his life several years earlier, he thought the illness "bad;" but the cancer had led to a deepening of his relationship with God and loved ones, and he had thought that "good." The chemotherapy he went through he thought "bad," and yet it led to his being free of cancer and that seemed "good." The treatment may have caused his congestive heart failure. Was the chemotherapy "bad" or "good?" "...I am no longer very good at telling the difference between good things and bad things."

May's words resonated with me. Loss of being mothered, thought "bad," seemed to have contributed to empathy for others, desire for their fullness of life, and cross-generation grieving—all now thought "good." The death of my marriage and the despair, thought "bad," led to trust in life, faith, and unexpected joy. Mom's illness and resulting dementia—"bad?"— led her to freedom from long-held defenses and fear, to an ability to receive and offer love, and to peace and trust. Accompanying Mom through multiple medical crises, paranoia, and dementia— "bad?"—led to a whole new life-giving relationship with Mom, this new depth of serenity and acceptance, and our many steps toward simply being. I now more willingly embraced our poverty of knowledge. I no longer was so tempted to label the events of my life as "good" or "bad."

Mortality

I realized, too, that death—mortality—had lost much of its sting. The fears surrounding thoughts of my own death were mostly gone. Not once during this new journey with Mom had my old whirlpool image emerged and threatened me with non-existence. Could I be at peace with my own mortality?

I had shed no tears at Mom's death, unlike the tears that flowed freely when Dad died and my turmoil about the seeming anguish of his dying. Dare I say it? I saw beauty in Mom's dying—her radiance, the trust with which she stepped into whatever lies beyond. And I saw this in someone whose fearfulness had cast a shadow over most of my life. She, who had feared death so much even two years earlier, had come to be at peace with mortality. What a precious legacy Mom had given me—her calm and trusting acceptance of dying.

I realized that I, too, had undergone several dyings during our journey, as I let go of old defenses and attempts to control. I had been immersed in emotions that had greatly troubled me in the past: sorrow, grief, aloneness, uncertainty, longing. Yet amidst these deaths and difficult feelings, I had found peace.

I wondered what form the rest of my life would take. What if I traveled into dementia? Would I continue to sense a loving presence with me? Would I remember the lessons of this time? I thought again of an article by Jane Thibault I'd read years earlier. She presents a fictional account of the diary entries over six weeks of a woman just diagnosed with an early stage of Alzheimer's disease.

The woman writes repeatedly of her fear of losing her memory of God. If I lose my memory of you, how can I love you? How can I serve you? Will you reject me, if I forget you?

While waiting for an appointment with her doctor, the diary writer conversed with a young woman who worked as a nurse's aide in a dementia unit. In the course of their conversation, the aide told about one of her patients who had asked her, "Honey, what's my name?" After being answered, the woman pointed to the crucifix on the wall of her room and said clearly and with a laugh, "Honey, most of the time I don't even know who I am; but he does, and that's all that counts."

Through this story, God had talked to the diary writer, assuring her that all would be well. She ends with the prayer: "In my dimmest moments, please let me witness to your loving care. Let me point to your cross and say to all who need to hear, 'I don't know who I am, but he does—and that's all that counts!' And let me say it lightly and with a laugh!"

Her prayer became mine. I trust that the glimpses I have had of sacred mystery's presence and action in Mom's life, even in her dementia, will continue to be lessons for me if I, too, travel this path.

Even if dementia plays no role in my march toward death, I likely will experience some restrictions: over where I go, whom I am with, how I move about and how well I can care for myself, perhaps how I think and feel, where I live, and what I can read and understand. How will I handle the loss of the everyday control that I take so for granted now? Will I gracefully let go at each step, trust in the loving presence I call "God," and sense that presence with me always? I believe the lessons of this time with Mom will come to my aid.

New Images

Two new images kept floating into consciousness during these weeks following Mom's death. In one vision I am floating in a wave-filled ocean. I suspect Thomas Greene's words in *When the Well Runs Dry* helped shape this image. He writes about floating in the limitless sea of God's mercy. Floating—not swimming, striving, or trying to control the direction of movement—but continuously opening to the current and adjusting one's movements so as to be in alignment with the sea's currents, with God's self-giving love flowing in all that exists. His words brought back memories of learning how to float as a young child in the ocean off Long Island, how to ease into and trust the support of the water that was so often turbulent and unpredictable. Easing into the water without knowing what the next moment would bring.

They brought to mind, too, a time at the ocean with my grandfather when I was a young adult. In the past I had recounted this event as an adventure tale. Now it took on a whole new meaning. The two of us had driven to Jones Beach. It must have been off-season; few others were around and no lifeguards. The surf along the southern coast of Long Island can be quite rough, but I was eager to take a dip. Grandpa decided not to join me but stood on the shore to watch over me. The surf was different from anything I had ever experienced. I was quickly drawn into water over my head and unable to swim back toward shore. The current was too strong to fight. It pulled me in a path roughly parallel to the shore. I stopped struggling and found myself swimming/floating with my eyes fixed on my grandfather's face, as he walked along the shore to keep abreast of me. He kept his face always turned toward me. I remember the strength and calm I felt as I focused on him and his unhurried pace. There was no panic or fear that I can remember, on his part or mine. I have no idea how long this continued or how far we traveled, but my guess is that we went at least a mile. Suddenly I felt a change in the pull of the current and found that I could work with it and slowly make my way toward the shore. When I reached land and Grandpa, he simply hugged me; and we walked back, retracing the long way we had come. Later, as we exited the beach, we discovered that warnings had been posted since we entered, against swimming due to the rip currents. This memory, which I can still feel in my body, I now saw as such a concrete illustration of what is possible, even amidst unpredictable turbulence, when one turns from fear, opens one's senses to the current, trusts in floating, and remains oriented toward love.

The second image I suspect arose from a recurrent prayer of mine—"May I be the song uttered in my creation"—and a poem by the Sufi mystic, Hafiz:

"I am
A hole in a flute
That the Christ's breath moves through—
Listen to this
Music."

I first learned of Hafiz' words from Carol Crumley, one of the leaders of my pilgrimage to Iona. She slipped them to me on a piece of paper shortly after I had played my flute in worship from the alcove above the altar of Iona's Abbey. They had stayed with me.

I saw myself as a flute offering music. This vision may have spoken especially to me since I am a flutist. I know in my body the mystery of how music emerges when I give myself fully over to the breath, the movements of my whole body, the play of my fingers on the flute, and all the sensory impressions of each note and phrase of the emergent music. The music arises and unfolds in a way unknown beforehand, as all of me flows in harmony with the life force and score given from something or somebody beyond me.

These new images spoke of the peacefulness I had discovered in myself and of what the words "simply being" were leading me toward. The trustworthy flow of water, or breath, stood in the place of the fearful turbulence of my old whirlpool. Sensing the flow and going with it had replaced my struggling and crying out for help.

Part VI: Beyond Death

Continuing Together

Mom's death did not bring an end to our journey together. Daily I continued to hold Mom in prayer, without words, without requests—just lovingly holding her. I had never before prayed for anyone who had died. I was surprised to be doing this, but it felt natural and right.

Slowly, the number of deceased people I prayed for expanded. I added my maternal grandfather first, in gratitude for his keeping love alive in me and in Mom, then his wife (my grandmother) and Dad, and then Dad's parents. I now hold in prayer all those deceased relatives I have known during my lifetime. Each has shaped in some way my life story, one that I now accept and honor.

Mom also continued in my daily life through a variety of concrete symbols. Her ashes were close beside me for two years. They rested in my writing room, with an "angel of remembrance" standing nearby. After we completed family discussions about where to place her ashes, I buried them, with a simple prayer ritual, at the foot of a red maple tree given in her honor by two of my former students. The tree stands on a rise before my home, placed so that I can see it—from my kitchen, my bed, and the living room's sitting area.

A stone also marks the spot. I found it during a retreat in New York State, the state where Mom and I lived the longest during my growing up. I stumbled upon it on one of my walks along the roads surrounding the retreat house. It is a simple gray, oval-shaped stone with a strain of white rock running completely through it, dividing it into two portions of unequal size. The white cleavage is a symbol of the past brokenness of our relationship. The rock's wholeness despite the cleavage speaks of our deep healing. The larger gray portion I think of as Mom and all the ancestors before her. It is "engraved" with a number of mysterious interconnecting lines that remind me of all that remains unknown about how past generations helped shape our journey. The smaller portion stands for me with my children and their children. It has a pointed end that looks forward toward the generations to come.

I felt Mom's presence with me, too, as I shared with others the story of our journey. As the first anniversary of Mom's death approached, Jeannene and I began to plan a retreat we would co-facilitate where I would offer a written version of our story.

I had joined a small writers' group several months earlier, just three of us who were writing memoirs that touched on spiritual issues. They were the first strangers who heard pieces of our journey. At first it was scary. They were more accomplished writers than I. What would they think of my writing skills? Also, I was revealing much more about myself than I ever had with near strangers. What if they criticized or discounted my writing—or me?

Month by month, I became more at ease. And each month they pushed me to bring even more of myself—especially my very young self—into the writing. I resisted for several months, but relented when we each agreed to write ten pages about our early years for our next meeting. We were to start with when and where we were born and see what followed. My ten pages easily turned into thirty. And, to my surprise, these pages could be woven into the story I had written about the new journey with Mom.

I now see, although I did not then, that part of my resistance was shying away from doing any writing that could possibly be viewed as feeling sorry for myself, or telling family secrets. After all, one of the lessons of my childhood was: "Do not feel sorry for yourself. Others have it worse. Deny sorrow, anger...." I had now written of events and troubling emotions that I had not spoken of previously to others.

This was another lesson in letting go of the old. The new

writing brought freedom to speak my truth to others, to share more of my inner self. It was as if I were singing. Since early childhood I had seldom sung out loud, and then only hesitantly and softly. An elementary school music teacher had suggested that I just mouth the words to songs, and I had taken her advice to heart. But now I was beginning to open my mouth wide and let music flow out.

The weekend retreat took place in a quiet country setting, with a small group. I sent out my writing two weeks beforehand, asking others to ponder how this tale might connect with their lives. Our story, entitled "Lessons in Simply Being," would not be the focus of the retreat; but hopefully it would be leaven for their going deeper into their own lives and freeing their imaginations about what might be possible. My journey with my mother, I suggested, was a story of living the unimaginable.

"How can we be freer to recognize the unimaginable when it begins to occur in our lives?" I asked. "How can we become more open to responding in ways that enable us to co-create with God the inconceivable?"

We began by sharing reflections prompted by my writing. Later, we thought about biblical stories of the unimaginable and engaged in art activities that might help us express desires we hadn't dared to believe possible. Looking through magazines, we found images we could arrange in collages to express our desires and the barriers to realizing them. We also rested in prolonged periods of silence and journaling.

After the retreat, I offered "Lessons in Simply Being" to close friends. Often they asked if they could share the writing with others. I found myself saying "yes" without hesitation. I felt again the freedom, the spacious joyfulness, of singing out loud. Sharing our story seemed so right—as a way of honoring Mom and a way we humans offer more life to one another. I was offering a song of praise, a celebration of the wondrous gift of life and of God with us.

I also felt Mom's presence beside me as I lived another unexpected story shortly after her death—a healing in my relationship with Dave.

New Healing

Dave and I had maintained a cordial relationship for several years. We worked well together around issues concerning our children, got together periodically for meals or walks, and had even spent Christmases together. I thought I had forgiven him and that much healing had taken place in me around the deep wound of his leaving our marriage. About four months after Mom's death, he had sent an email message from Brazil announcing his intention to marry the woman he had been dating. I celebrated how well I handled this news. I did not dwell in the old place of fearing myself unlovable. There still was a good deal I did not understand about how he could leave our marriage or about what I, or our marriage, meant to him; but I thought I had let go of needing to know.

Two months later, I had lunch with my son. Brett had emailed me a few days earlier about his and Ellie's latest wedding plan— to invite close family members to spend a week together at the North Carolina coast that would culminate in their marriage at the ocean's edge. I went to lunch eager to hear more.

In the midst of all our catching up, Brett turned to his wedding plans and said, "Mom, I really want you to be fully involved in all the planning and all the activities leading up to the wedding."

"There's no way in hell that I am going to spend a week in the same house with your dad and his new wife." The words just flew out of my mouth.

Wow! Where had that come from? The words and their tone violated my firm intention to never put Brett or Lisa between their dad and me, and every desire I had for how to support them as they dealt with their issues about his marriage. Clearly I had more soul-searching to do.

My own words haunted me as I searched for their source and

meaning. What came quickly to mind was a recent meeting I'd had with Dave. Soon after his return from Brazil, he invited me to lunch, our first opportunity to talk since the email message announcing his plans to marry. I suspect I went to this meeting with my antennae out and quivering, hoping to gather more information about what it all meant. What did this say about the thirty years of our marriage, and me? He had said when he left that he thought he was unable to live with anyone.

We never came close to discussing these concerns. Dave talked at length about his stay in Brazil. I listened and asked questions. After a half hour with no questions about me and my life, I did something uncharacteristic. I broke in on his story. "Maybe you'd like to know what has been going on with me."

Without waiting for an answer, I launched into an account of my recent steps toward retirement, visits with the kids, and so on—all activities at the surface of my life, but nothing about my reactions to his marriage announcement. We ended without addressing, or even glancing at, the elephant sitting on the table between us.

I had found our meeting unsettling. But it was only as I replayed it in my memory that I realized just how upset I was and why. Despite all the new lessons, I was still stuck in the old pattern with Dave. I enabled interactions that were both hurtful to me and untruthful. I had ceded virtually all power to him, eager to glean from his words and actions information about our past marriage and me. I hadn't dared to ask for what I wanted, or to say anything about the questions his announcement had raised.

I did not like what I had uncovered—what it said about me, or Dave. So I postponed his request for another meeting. I went off, in turmoil over this new discovery, to a long-planned silent retreat.

During the retreat's first three days, within the periods of communal centering prayer, quiet openness alternated with flashbacks of interactions with Dave that had been painful at the time. But I didn't feel pain or turmoil as these scenes floated into the quiet. I just let them be, without grasping or trying to work with them. They drifted into the deep silence of prayer and then drifted out again. After our prayer times, I usually took a long walk. As I strode along, words began to emerge about things I might say to Dave. I let the sentences simply rise into consciousness and then leave. My gratefulness grew. Some deep healing felt in process.

At other times during these first days, I revisited the pain of feeling my love neither received nor reciprocated by Dave. In all the years since his leaving, I had not heard anything he had valued about our marriage, or me, except how we had reared our children. Had he received nothing else?

I reexamined, too, the puzzle of why he left. From early in our marriage, I had seen his difficulty in knowing what he wanted — in life, in daily decisions, in our relationship. I had tried, and failed, to help him find and voice his desires. Asking about or listening for his wishes hadn't worked. So I had fallen back on my childhood pattern of attentively watching, trying to infer how to please. In the absence of other information, I tried to offer him what I would want in similar circumstances. I knew the family life I desired for our children and worked to make it happen, at times pulling Dave away from his work. Had that felt too controlling, or confining? If I had been able then to trustingly flow with the moment, could Dave have found his way without leaving?

He was the one adult I thought loved me and yet he had chosen to leave, knowing the pain he would cause. How could anyone who cared for me at all do this? The words, "I didn't deserve that," emerged for the first time. This simple assertion felt an integral part of claiming my own integrity, the truth of who I am.

The fourth day brought new experiences within the

communal prayer times. In early morning prayer, images floated in of sacred love as a large ball of fire embracing all that exists, and of me as a small flame offering love. The two fused. I knew myself as "beloved," and as a participant in the flow of mercy.

At a later prayer period that day, there was just silence and wide-awake alertness—a sense of being at a point of absolute stillness and clarity. From that time on, there were no more flashbacks of interactions with Dave.

On the sixth day, I took a long walk after morning prayer. The stroll away from the retreat house was like those of previous days, a time of savoring all that was in the moment: the movements of my limbs, the wind, open meadows, wildflowers, the dark silence of the woods, the stream, the gravel beneath my feet, the butterflies and dragonflies that accompanied me. But something new happened as I turned to retrace my steps. A dialogue with Dave began to play out within me. I tried, as I had earlier when such words emerged, to let them float by and away. But this time they did not. They continued without any effort on my part. By the time the retreat house came into view I had found the words—or they had found me—that felt just right for speaking my truth.

A burst of freedom enveloped me as I wrote in my journal. I was speaking from my heart. And I was not trying to control what, if anything, might come from the words—even whether I would ever speak them to Dave. It was enough right now to know the words. Throughout the remaining two days of the retreat, the Dave-and-me issues were absent. Something important felt complete.

I did speak these words to Dave a few days after returning home, in an email message. They told of things I had never so clearly and openly shared with him: the depth of the pain I experienced during the years of despair, the new life I was now living, and my forgiveness of him. Then I added:

Why am I saying this now? Because after our last time together I suddenly realized that I did not want to participate in such an interaction ever again. I saw clearly that I had been an enabler of conversations with you that did not feel truthful. Here we were. You recently had emailed me that you were to be married. You had broken the promise of marriage to me and were about to make that commitment to someone else. And the clearest statement I had heard at your leaving me was that you thought you could not live with anyone. There certainly was a big elephant trumpeting between us, but neither of us spoke about it. You recounted your travails in finding funding to return to Brazil, and I listened sympathetically and tried to offer a helpful suggestion or two. You did not ask about my life, but I did break in eventually and say a few things about what was going on at its surface—but nothing about the depths. And then we left.

Replaying this time, I saw an old, old pattern of interaction; and I did not like what it said about either of us. I realized that I needed to look clear-eyed at my role, and at you. I needed to become clearer about what I would want in any future interactions....

Is friendship possible for us? I really do not know. I offer only a few thoughts as a start for us to look more clearly at what's possible. First, the deep hurt of your leaving is a wound that remains a part of our interactions. I understand it better, deal with it differently, and so on—but it still is there.

Second, I do not yet know whether I can trust you. I certainly cannot place the faith in you that I did earlier, nor do I wish to. But I am aware that I act defensively with you. Greater trust I would hope could develop if we can engage in straightforward interactions with one another, clarify our expectations about how we interact, and fulfill these at least most of the time.

Third, although you have used the term "friendship" to describe our relationship of the past few years, I would not call it that. For me, being a friend means keeping in touch, caring that each other's life is going well, and expressing that caring in both words and actions. I think we have been acting more like cordial acquaintances or distant family members, interacting pleasantly when we happen to have contact but otherwise thinking little of one another.

So, I want to ask you to ponder what you hope for in our future interactions. Do you really want friendship? If so, why? What does that mean to you? If not, what do you want? I will do the same, and then perhaps we can begin to talk more honestly with one another about our future.

Another surge of freedom and gratitude flowed through me as I sent the message. I had broken free from the old pattern. Earlier I had come to be myself with Mom, but her dementia meant that I had not been able to speak my truth to her in words. With Dave I could. And I did not frame the words to please him, or otherwise try to control whether or how he might respond. It was enough to just say the words.

Within a few days, Dave did respond. "I have…started to feel my way through your insights and deep reflections about us…I am interested in clarifying and sharing our expectations and experiences."

So we started on a new path. Our first meeting brought an open conversation about the death of our marriage and where we found ourselves now. Unexpectedly, I expressed a further issue for me: "I can't understand how anyone who cared for me at all could knowingly hurt me as much as you did." The tears came but also new freedom. In saying the words aloud, I finally felt able to let go of having to understand.

Dave, in turn, expressed more clearly than ever before, the depth of his "stuckness" at the time. And as he talked, I was able to hear some things he had valued about me. I had grieved so long that nothing of all those years of loving had been received or valued. I learned that something had.

In subsequent times together, we talked openly about his marriage plans, about Brett's wedding, even about the spiritual grounding he saw in me and felt missing in him. We enjoyed our times together; we even laughed and reminisced. Forgiveness felt more complete. The possibility of something like a "friendship" began to seem real.

When my marriage died and during the long years of my despair, Mom could offer no support, comfort, or even presence to me. But now she walked beside me, "mothering" me. All the fruits of our journey were part of the healing with Dave. They helped me discover and face the hidden brokenness of our relationship. They helped me take that brokenness to prayer and stay with what emerged. They helped me trust that I would be guided about whether and how to speak to Dave. And now, there was even more new fruit—a new, potentially life-enhancing relationship with Dave.

A New Chapter

When Lisa gave birth to her first child, a new chapter began in our family story. Isaac was another unimaginable happening. We all thought conception by the usual route not possible after Aaron's operations. Yet Isaac was conceived naturally. At first we held our breaths, scarcely daring to believe in this pregnancy. But all proceeded smoothly and by Christmas, as the first anniversary of Mom's death approached, we had begun to plan for Isaac's birth in early April.

Lisa and Aaron's visit with me that Christmas brought a delightful surprise. I knew I would be helping them around the birth, but Lisa had told me they did not yet know what they might need.

As Lisa recounted with laughter the story of her friend Julie's reaction to her birthing classes, one of Lisa's desires slipped out. Julie had been shown a video of her instructor giving birth.

"It was way more than Julie wanted to know about her instructor," Lisa exclaimed. "No one is going to be with me when I'm giving birth except Aaron and Mom."

Lisa and I immediately burst into smiles as we realized the invitation just uttered.

"Just tell me when to come," I replied. "I would love to be with you."

At three a.m. on Easter morning, Aaron called.

"It's time, Mom."

"I will be on the road at the break of dawn," I promised.

I prayed, packed, left messages to rearrange my schedule, and set off on the nine-hour trip at first light. As I drove through the mountains of North Carolina, Virginia, West Virginia, and Pennsylvania, all was shrouded in fog. The shapes of trees, boulders, and bluffs came into being as I drove toward them; yet all remained behind a veil. The fog, the mysteriously emerging forms, and the veil added to my sense that something wondrous was about to spring into life. One after another public radio station filled the car and my heart with the joyous music of Easter.

"Halleluiah."

When I entered Lisa's hospital room at three in the afternoon, the midwife called out: "You must be Lisa's mom. You're just in time. We are about to start pushing."

For the next three hours, we all worked together in the birthing. The midwife and Aaron supported Lisa's legs and helped her push and relax. I applied cold compresses to Lisa's head, offered sips of drink as needed, and kept the warming tray ready for Isaac. We cried out in wonder as we caught a first glimpse of the crown of Isaac's head. We praised Lisa and urged her onward. In shared hushed awe, we held our breath as Isaac's body slipped out of Lisa's.

We wept, hugged, and kissed one another as Isaac became more fully a member of his new world — as he cried, as he was wiped clean of his birthing fluids, as Aaron cut his umbilical cord, as he first took to the breast, and as he turned from blue to pink to fully-oxygenated red. We passed Isaac from one set of eager arms to the next. Cradling him, we leaned forward to gaze into his eyes and welcome him into our lives. Out of the fear and darkness of Aaron's cancer came the "miracle" of Isaac's conception, and now the joy of his birth on Easter day.

The next days were a blur of new tasks, new roles, new challenges, and exhaustion — yet days of happiness and wonder, too. I often sat beside Lisa as she nursed Isaac, delighting in how his deep desire for food was met so fully by Lisa's whole being. I felt in my own body the remembered sense of nursing my children, the profound bodily connection, and the satisfaction of being able to meet another's needs. I witnessed Lisa's love and skill in nurturing Isaac and her daily steps in learning more about the ways of this particular new being.

I returned home after nine days, but kept up daily with Isaac's doings. I knew from my visit that he suckled well, but that he was not otherwise an "easy baby." He slept little and cried a good deal. Now I listened to Lisa as his periods of inconsolable crying increased in frequency and length. I heard her distress about how often he appeared to be in pain. She added one after another restriction to her diet, hoping to make her breast milk more easily digestible. Nothing seemed to help. Then came prescriptions for treating acid reflux distress. The first medicine they tried helped a bit, but not all that much. Lisa, Aaron, and Isaac were all in distress.

Sharing her concerns with me by phone seemed to help Lisa, but I longed to offer more. When I looked at my schedule ahead, I found two week-long periods that I could free up for another visit. Perhaps I could help by being another lap, shoulder, and pair of hands.

"Yes! Come as soon as you can," she said, when I offered.

So after a little more than two weeks at home, I returned. Their time of great stress continued, but my extra lap and shoulder provided a few more periods of rest for Isaac—and all. A new, stronger medicine was being tried now. By the end of my week's visit, it seemed to promise more relief from pain.

A day before I left, Lisa and I stole away for an hour to shop for birthday gifts for each other. Our birthdays, and Mother's Day, would come shortly after I left. That evening, as I wrapped Lisa's present, I felt again how grateful I was for what I had seen in my daughter—her loving care of Isaac. I was seeing a new facet of Lisa's beauty and, at the same time, receiving a clear affirmation that the cycle of loss of mothering within our family had indeed been broken.

I had never spoken to Lisa about this cycle, or of my sense that I had broken it and been able to mother her and Brett. Suddenly, it seemed just the right time to share with her our family story. I wrote her a letter that expressed my appreciation for how she was nurturing Isaac. I shared my understanding of the past losses of mothering for her great-grandmother, her grandmother, and me, and spoke of my joy in how she was so clearly affirming that this cycle had been broken. I sealed the letter in an envelope and attached it to her birthday present with instructions to wait for her birthday before she opened either the present or letter. I suggested that she might want to read the letter in private. Early the next day I left for home, accompanied by my own cards and present from Lisa — and instructions to wait for my birthday and Mother's Day.

Lisa's birthday came first. She shared with me by phone her appreciation of my letter, although in a guarded way that I did not then understand. When I opened my Mother's Day card a week later, I understood. Lisa had chosen a Hallmark card whose front held a single golden flower in a vase composed of words piled on top of one another — words like "love," "comfort," "praise," and "teach." Inside the card, Lisa added her own words: "I am quickly developing a greater appreciation for all the wonderful mothering I have received and what a great gift it is. I only hope I can provide Isaac with that kind of nurturing. Thank you!"

Never before to my knowledge had Lisa or I used the word "mothering" with each other. Yet here it arose in each of us to express our appreciation for what we saw in the other. Now I understood the guardedness in Lisa's response to my letter. She was in awe of the congruence in our messages and did not want to spoil the surprise for me. We now could share our delight in what had transpired.

During these first months of Isaac's life, Lisa and I also plumbed other new depths in our relationship. We both now knew the wonder of harboring new life within our bodies and of giving birth to a new being — and the joys, distress, and responsibility of "mothering."

Once, as I sat beside Lisa while she nursed Isaac, I saw a look of awe transform her face. "This is forever, isn't it?" she said in a hushed voice.

"Yes," I said. We both knew what "this" was.

I like to imagine that Mom accompanied us in this new chapter to our family story—and that she was smiling and said, "Well done!"

Part VII: New Envisioning

Prayer and Daily Life

Changes in everyday life and in prayer are interwoven in the story I have told. At the time of Mom's death, I thought of prayer as separate from the rest of my day. When I looked back over the years, I saw the movements in these two distinct domains as intertwined in a dance of mutual influence. I was aware of some blurring of their boundary because years earlier I had read Brother David Steindle-Rast's book, *Gratefulness: The Heart of Prayer*. I was surprised that he used the word "prayer" to refer to the bursts of gratitude that co-occurred with the "gifts" in daily life. But I continued to think of prayer as a time set apart from the rest of life.

This vision began to alter dramatically the second summer after Mom's death, during a ten-day silent retreat. Embedded within each day's silence were several hours of communal centering prayer and long solitary walks. When invited at the opening gathering to share reflections on the question "What do you want?" I had no answer beyond the desire for simple receptivity. But I quickly came to a troubling discovery about myself.

During the first day or two, as I thought about whether to sign up to talk with one of the retreat facilitators, I became aware that I might want others to see me as "doing well" spiritually. I wanted to sign up, but why? I felt no need to talk about anything in particular. Was I clinging to a need to be "special" in my prayer life? I knew this need as part of my past life, when it had been so important to achieve in school and in my profession in order to assure myself that I was worthwhile and to convince others to pay attention to me and, yes, love me. Was I now trying to be an achiever in prayer?

Next I began to think about recent times of centering prayer. During some I had felt a very strong desire—a need?—to express my gratitude and love to God more and more. This, too, felt old, like trying to have enough to offer.

Finally, I found striving in how I used my sacred word "willing." At times I was using it more like a sledgehammer. I was trying to force being willing, rather than just expressing my intent and resting in it.

I was surprised, and dismayed, about this newly discovered arena of willfulness. How had the myths of control I had honed in daily life slipped into my prayer? Once I recognized the old patterns, I longed to let them go. So I did not sign up to talk with anyone. And, unexpectedly, I found myself reading about spiritual striving the very evening after I had discovered my own.

I had read Beatrice Bruteau's book, *The Easter Mysteries*, and was drawn especially to the later chapters. I sensed some important, but not-yet-fully-understood connections between my experiential journey and her more philosophical, metaphysical analysis of union with the sacred. I yearned to understand the links better, so I had brought her book to the retreat. The night after I discovered my striving in prayer, I read a chapter that talked about this very need to be special, this effort to achieve in the spiritual life.

I found a timely gift in her chapter, a "freedom prayer" that I adapted for my use. Whenever I caught myself striving in prayer, or feeling dismayed about it afterwards, I just prayed: "May I, dear God, be free of any need to be special or to achieve in my spiritual life." I would say it only once and then rest, trusting that freedom would come in time. It was not something I could make happen. When the striving or dismay reemerged, I would say the prayer once more and rest again. Only later did I realize how I was choosing, over and over again, to turn toward God rather than running with my own ego-driven thoughts and feelings. My freedom prayer, like centering prayer, was a way of expressing my intent to trust in the sacred.

Shortly after the discovery of my spiritual willfulness, a new "sacred word" came to me in prayer, the word "open." "Open" did not hold the striving I inadvertently had attached to "willing." Before each subsequent prayer period, I expressed my intent to be open, to be spaciously receptive; and then I rested in that intent.

For years I had sensed a loving presence during prayer. Usually I was quite aware of my own presence, too. I was engaged in something like a silent exchange of love, a dance, or a dialogue. Now I began to feel God's presence without any sense of my separate self. The only words that came to me after these times were "pulled into God." I experienced "being love or energy radiating outward." Later I recalled how others used the words "resting in God" to describe contemplative prayer. These felt right, too.

One evening, I was reading Bruteau's words about God's invisibility and ours, too, once we are stripped of all our attachments. An image emerged that captured something of the new prayer experiences. It built upon Thomas Merton's words about the false self:

"I wind experiences around myself and cover myself with pleasures and glory like bandages in order to make myself perceptible to myself and to the world, as if I were an invisible body that could only become visible when something visible covered its surface."

In the scene that emerged for me, I was being unwrapped of those cloaks that I had associated with myself: the hiding of what might bother others, the need to reduce others' fears and anger, the doing, the striving, the need to be "good" or "special," the fear of being unlovable. As the unwrapping progressed, I became invisible. All there was, was God. The essence of me was indistinguishable from sacred mystery, and from all being. I had a sense of my invisible self, dancing within the invisibility of the divine.

My earlier image of floating in a sea of mercy also changed in an important way. I no longer saw myself floating upon the sea. Rather, I was floating *within* that sea, within love, indistinguishable in my essence from the sea.

Only late in the retreat did I connect the new prayer experiences and the images they had birthed to one of the wonders of Isaac's being. When I had last seen Isaac, he was three and a half months old and no longer crying inconsolably. He readily smiled at folks and laughed. But what especially caught my attention and filled me with awe was what I call his "love looks." They occurred in the minutes right after nursing. Isaac lay still, at complete rest, but with eyes wide open, bright and sparkling, and with a face that expressed utter delight as he looked deep into our eyes. His mouth took the form of a gentle open smile, but there was nothing of the active excitement and laughter of other times of smiling. I experienced him as radiating love to us from a place of deep peace. I felt I was seeing and basking in sacred love. Lisa, Aaron, and I—we all came to delight in these moments.

Recalling Isaac's "love looks" brought back memories of these same looks in Brett and Lisa as infants. I looked again at the picture I had found when I went through the belongings Mom left behind—a large framed photo of me at just about Isaac's age. I was radiating the same "love look."

These looks seemed to show so clearly that of God at the heart of each of us—love as our very essence. Could it be that as young babies our essence is not yet hidden by all the defenses, or layers of ego, we develop so early in life—by Merton's wrappings? Because of all these coverings, we require so many lessons in letting go before our essence can shine forth once again. Perhaps it is only when we again become as open and unguarded as young infants that we experience and radiate to others the paradise of the unconditional love and peace that lies within. I now thought this might have been what I saw in Mom during her final months, what I then called her "radiance."

The retreat time held yet another important learning for me. I experienced how the openness to sacred mystery I was experiencing in prayer could become one with all my life. As I moved more toward non-striving in prayer, I found myself moving more deeply into receptive presence in other ways, too—in working, eating, reading, savoring the natural world, and in exercise.

Most days I walked a mile or two along the roads around the retreat house. The roads were narrow, winding, and heavily traveled by cars and trucks. At first I was disappointed, worried about the passing traffic. I found these walks distracting, far from peaceful. On the seventh day, however, as I moved along the same path as on previous days, I suddenly became aware of how very different my walk had become. My breaths were longer, more even, and more spaced. I was much more aware of the feel of my body in motion and of the changing sensations of air against my skin (from breezes and passing vehicles) and of the shifts in temperature as I moved from light to deep shade to sunlight. Simultaneously, I heard more sounds (of birds, insects, the moving trees and grasses, children at play and adults building a house), and the variations in sound produced by different vehicles. I was seeing so much more of what was present in each moment—more of the shapes and color of the gravel at my feet, more of birds, insects, animals, and humans, more of the changing cloud patterns and colors of the sky, more of the different grasses, shrubs, and trees and of the fruit they bore. More of everything.

I no longer focused on the passing cars or trucks, or plotted my course of action. I sensed their approach and seemingly unconsciously adjusted my pace and location on the road without losing any of the other sensations that filled my awareness. I was more alive and present during this walk than I had been before. I was moving with the flow rather than defending myself against it or trying to control it.

Upon my return home, the openness and non-striving I experienced in prayer continued to permeate more and more of my life. I realized, too, that offering spiritual direction helped erase the distinction between prayer and daily life. I was actively listening to and responding to another. Yet at the same time, I was in a place of prayer, of simple open presence. As more people came to me for spiritual guidance, my days became punctuated with these times of human interaction immersed within prayer. This aided me, much as the liturgy of hours does within monastic life, in regularly turning to and resting in the sacred throughout the course of daily life.

Prayer was no longer only a self-consciously set-aside time for God. Increasingly it was pervading all of my life.

Old Memories – New Insight

During the same summer that led to this new vision of prayer, the "past" also became alive for me in a new way. Twice, within the span of just two months, old memories mysteriously reappeared in a new pattern and led to insights around old wounds.

The Great Egret and Mom's Grieving

For the first time since Mom's death, I revisited some of our troubling conversations during her dementia. I hadn't written about them; probably I hadn't wanted to remember. They had made Mom and me very sad. One talk went something like this:

"Where's Bill?" Mom would demand with urgency, and agitation.

"Mom, you're having trouble remembering that Dad died several years ago. That's why he isn't here with you now."

"Oh," Mom would sigh and begin to weep. "How did he die?"

"You and Dad drove to my home for Christmas, and we had a fun time all together. Brett and Lisa were home. And Bill Jr. and his family were with us, too. But after Christmas, Dad came down with a bad cold. Despite all our care, he developed pneumonia...." I then would recount the story of his time in the hospital, our daily visits, and Dad's death.

"How sad," Mom might say amidst her tears. "I miss him."

"Yes, I know. We had a lovely memorial service for Dad at my church...."

A week later, a similar conversation would play out. Again Mom's face would contort with pain. And she would cry and express sorrow over her loss.

After three or four of these talks, I made a memory book for

Mom. I put in it the newspaper notice of Dad's death, the program from his memorial service, and the poem that Mom had asked us to read at the service. In response to subsequent "Where's Bill?" inquiries, we would look at the book as I told her about his death and the service. Sometimes I read one of the scripture passages, the pastor's statement of comfort, or the Baha'i prayer Lisa had offered. Or I would name the hymns I played on my flute. We might even hum a line or two of one of her favorites. But I always ended by reciting the poem. It was what Mom responded to most—what she wanted to hear.

She and Dad had treasured this poem. Uncle George, Mom's brother-in-law, had written it while grieving the loss of his son, born just a year after me. He had committed suicide in his twenties, and Uncle George had been the one to find him.

> "I saw a leaf fall today—early.
> Why?
> I know not.
> I wish I knew.
>
> "I saw this one particular leaf
> flutter down
> and my heart fell with it."

Before I finished reciting just these first few lines, the tears always came. And after the poem ended, Mom would clasp the memory book to her chest. From time to time she would open it and silently turn pages. Embracing and reengaging it seemed to comfort her. Several minutes later, her thoughts would light upon something else and the tears would stop.

To be truthful, I dreaded these talks. It seemed cruel for Mom to have to rediscover her loss over and over again, and feel raw pain anew. But these talks continued until just a few months before her death.

I found myself reliving our "Where's Bill?" conversations at Sunset Beach on the North Carolina coast. I had taken a long early morning walk to the end of the barrier island where the water wrapped around from ocean to marsh. This was a special place for me. I often sat here among the birds, sensing them— their colors and shapes, sounds, and activities—together with the music of the surf, and the feel of sun, sand, and wind on my body. Here, too, I often just sat in silent prayer.

I was the only human on this stretch of sand. I walked to the marsh side and sat with my back against a small dune, looking out at the marsh. I had barely settled, when a great egret alighted at the water's edge, just twenty feet in front of me. My heart swelled. Egrets, and all herons, had long been for me symbols of the sacred. "...in the shadow of your wings I sing for joy" (Psalm 63.7). This verse had been with me ever since I discovered my new life of faith. And these words, placed beneath a picture of a heron in flight, graced the program for my "coming to faith" service.

All my senses opened wide to this great egret. Its lean body glowed in the sunlight, throwing white light upon the blue-brown water behind and the sand stretching between the two of us. For twenty minutes I remained transfixed by the egret, as it stood rooted in the sandy muck at the marsh's edge. The bird stretched its graceful neck toward the heavens and then bowed toward the water, toward the food of daily life. Again and again, stretch and bow. The stretching and bowing mirrored my own yearning to lose myself in the sacred, and yet to remain grounded in each moment of my everyday life.

Into this time with the egret floated memories of the "Where's Bill?" conversations. I had no idea why they came then. I had not been thinking about Mom, or anything related to her. But now one after another of our talks floated into and then out of the peacefulness of the moment. It was as if I were serenely observing a movie. All the memories were there, readily accessible. They were replaying for me in the stillness of this time.

And then a new movie began to play—one from the months immediately after Dad's death, when Mom still had her memory and thought faculties. These were different conversations between Mom and me. I hadn't thought of them for at least seven years. They had taken place four or more years before our "Where's Bill?" talks, at a time when Mom was caught in her fear and I was trying to make everything all right.

"Why can't I cry?" Mom would ask. "What's wrong with me? It's not right."

"Maybe you're still in something like shock, Mom," I'd say. "Just be gentle with yourself and give yourself time. You are adjusting to so many new things all at once."

None of my attempts to reassure her helped. When she kept raising these concerns, I asked my pastor to visit and talk with Mom about grieving. Mom enjoyed the visit, but still the tears didn't flow. Nor did the visit calm her. Later, Mom agreed to talk about her distress with the social worker at her assisted living home—a courageous move for her. I arranged for a series of such talks, but again no tears and no comfort.

"Why can't I cry?" and other expressions of distress continued for several months, but the tears never came. Eventually Mom no longer uttered the questions aloud, but I suspected she still asked them.

As this second reel of memories played on, an insight suddenly emerged, bringing together the two sets of memories in a way I had never before entertained. Our "Where's Bill?" talks in dementia might have helped Mom, at long last, grieve Dad's death. The tears and sorrow that welled up each time Mom rediscovered his death may not have been cruel at all. They may have enabled her to finally feel and express her grief, in measured doses, and remain with her grief long enough to find her way to the peace within.

Joy filled me at the very moment I realized this possibility.

After several minutes of savoring gratitude, I stood and bowed deeply to the egret. I turned and began to retrace my steps along the beach, at the surf's edge. A thankfulness song, something like one of Winnie the Pooh's spontaneous ditties, burst forth from me. And I did a little dance step amidst the scurrying sandpipers.

This new thought — this possibility — felt so right.

Conversations with Mom that had pained me were now transformed into interactions that had helped her find peace. And reliving these two sets of conversations together had thrown into sharp relief the transformation that had occurred in each of us. Mom had become able to experience her grief, while still feeling love around her and knowing peace. Her old defenses and looking to me to make it all right had disappeared. And I had become able to accompany her calmly in her distress. No longer was I protecting myself from her emotions or trying to prove myself lovable.

Suddenly, another insight arose. We both had been learning, at similar points in time, how to stay with grief and find the peace within it — Mom in her grieving of Dad's death, and I in my grieving of our loss of being mothered. Gerald May's words came to me again: "...I am no longer very good at telling the difference between good things and bad things."

Some Unfinished Business?

Another set of relived memories arose barely a month later and addressed the wound of Dave's leaving me. It had been a year since I'd sent the email to Dave in which I broke free of our old patterns. Despite all the healing, I was living — I thought peacefully — with some unanswered questions. Why had he left? How could I think our marriage good, and yet Dave leave? How could he hurt me so? I believed I had let go of needing answers.

Then old memories of Dave reappeared, not at the beach or in meditation upon some aspect of nature, but in centering prayer.

Two memories of Dave drifted into the deep quiet of prayer and then out again. I had no idea why they appeared just then. I was not aware of thinking about Dave, or his painful departure from our marriage. Their appearance surprised me, but even more, the surge of empathy and love for Dave that flowed through me in response.

The first memory was of words that had startled me during a counseling session before he first left. Seemingly out of the blue, with no context given either before or later, he had said:

"Maybe I'm a sociopath."

I remembered rushing in: "Of course, you're not."

Yet now I was rehearing his words. I wasn't grasping at them in search of understanding, or rushing to "fix it." I just heard them anew, and let them be.

Next, scenes of Dave's increasing depression, during the year leading up to his final leaving, floated into the deep silence. Despite my attempts to gently probe, he had not been able to talk with me about the depression. Nor had he talked about it during our counseling sessions. I found myself reliving these scenes without any effort to understand, or to help Dave feel better. I just felt a surge of empathy and love flow out of me toward him.

Then rest and stillness filled the remainder of the prayer time.

An hour later, as I wrote in my journal, two further memories came to mind unsolicited — and some new understanding of what was happening within me. First I relived a scene of one of our conversations after Dave left. I was expressing pain and anger, when Dave's eyes suddenly filled with tears. "I have failed," he said, with eyes averted and head hung low.

I had responded heatedly with something like: "I can't understand why you won't fight for this family."

Next, the memory arose of a story Dave had recounted to me early in our marriage. It was the story of a good man holding a lion cub protectively under his jacket, even as the cub tore at the flesh of his chest. His dad had told this story, more than once, as a lesson about the importance of faithfulness. And he had told it in the context of his wife's, Dave's mother's, slow death from cancer. Dave had received it, and passed it on to me, as a morality tale.

I had never before put these four memories together. Just as suddenly as the memories appeared, they led me to understand for the first time how hard leaving had been for Dave. Yes, he had known a good deal about how much he would be hurting me. But now I knew how much he hadn't wanted to. *His anguish as he declared, "Maybe I am a sociopath."* He had cared for me and wanted to be faithful. *His return after his first leaving. The year of increasing depression before he left for good. The tears and "I have failed."* After all these years, I finally connected with Dave's pain, and could feel empathy and love for him. I still didn't understand his need to leave. But I could feel and respond to his suffering.

Although these memories of Dave had been available for years, perhaps I had not been accessible to them. Far more immediate to me had always been *my* pain, and my struggle to believe that Dave had loved me. Now that I no longer *needed* him as a partner in life, as proof I was lovable, or as the purveyor of the truth about our relationship, I was free to see his pain, feel it, and offer love. No longer did I need to resent or judge him, or defend myself against him.

I wrote in my journal that day: "Can I raise these memories with Dave and my new sense of their meaning? I will listen to Spirit."

Over the next two weeks, I held all that had happened with deep gratitude. Then Dave suggested a breakfast meeting. I went, not knowing whether I would say anything about my new understanding. But, midway through our breakfast, it felt right to say something. I recounted the four memories that had arisen and said:

"They helped me see, more clearly than ever before, how hard it was for you to leave me."

I could see by Dave's face that these words meant a great deal to him. "Yes," he said in a very quiet voice. "It was very hard. I kept not wanting to; and yet something kept pulling me away. Our marriage was good. It was all good. I didn't understand why I kept feeling this need to leave, why I couldn't just stay...."

Here was affirmation of his pain—and much more. I heard from him, for the very first time, that our marriage had been good. His leaving had profoundly shaken my confidence in my own view. His words "it was good" meant a great deal to me. By some "miracle," we now were helping to heal one another. We each were able to go beyond our own pain and offer love.

As I pondered all that had just transpired, I remembered a question my writing coach had posed just a few months earlier. She was probing for some new topics I might write about.

"Is there some unfinished business with Dave?"

Where had that come from, I thought. I had not suggested any such thing. Didn't she see all the healing that had taken place? Inside, I felt myself digging in my heels and shouting "no, no, no." That alone should have been a clue.

I had said nothing in reply, and had promptly crossed off this topic as a possibility. But there was unfinished business—and the finishing Dave and I did together has been life-giving for each of us.

These tales underscore once again that the unimaginable is possible. The "past" can become very much alive and offer new life in the "present."

Who's Family?

Shortly after living these two tales, I found myself reviewing my entire life with a seemingly simple question in mind—Who is my family?

The story I have told is about family, about people bound together by biological and marital ties. It is a tale of transformation within this family. Mutual nurturing and love replaced missed mothering. Fear transformed into peace. The agony of divorce gave way to empathy and a surprising new friendship. But in the living of this family story, new visions of family emerged. And they have continued to evolve, transforming my sense of loss and scarcity.

As a child I often felt without family. In adolescence, my desire for family became longing for a man who would love me and want to companion me in life. We would have children and form a family like the vision I had drawn from my high school friend. We would face together the hard things life threw our way.

Dave and I did create the family I so wanted. It was the supporting framework of my life for almost thirty years. But when Dave left, that family fell apart—and my life, too.

During the years of despair, I began to form new visions of family. Brett and Lisa helped me see that the three of us still were a loving family, only a one-parent version. Then came the realization that this small unit might expand one day, as Brett and Lisa brought their partners into my family. This possibility first became real to me as I sat on the lawn at Tanglewood listening to a summer performance of the Boston Symphony Orchestra. Brett and I had been visiting Lisa at her college in Massachusetts. We were getting to know Lisa's boyfriend Aaron and beginning a friendship with his mother, with whom we were staying for the week. Now here we were picnicking together, sharing music, food, laughter, and stories of our lives. Suddenly I could envision my tiny three-person family expanding through marriages and births—a vision that grew into reality as Lisa and Aaron married, then Brett and Ellie, and Isaac entered the world. And both Lisa and Brett married into large extended families that opened their arms to me.

But a different vision also began to form in me during the years of despair—family as a web of meaningful human connections. My web had Brett and Lisa, and their future partners and children, close beside me at the center, with thick threads joining us all to one another. When close friends and spiritual companions entered my life, I envisioned them, too, as nearby in the web and connected to me by threads that thickened as our friendships grew. My brother and his family, my church community, and some of my academic colleagues were more distant from me and connected to me with less thick threads. Experiencing all the support my children and I received around my operation stretched this vision to encompass more and more people. Family was no longer based on biological ties and marriage, but on nurturing and loving relationships—wherever they emerged.

Margaret Guenther suggests in *Toward Holy Ground* that one of the central tasks for "the second half of life" is redefining family. This web was my redefinition. And the new vision was immensely comforting. It addressed my fears. I did have loving companions in life. I can rely on this web, I thought. And my trust in this web grew over the years, as the number of people connected to me with thick threads increased.

But then, I began to experience the reality that the center of my web, those bound to me with thick threads, could not be relied upon to stay fixed in place and function. This realization struck forcefully when Beth, a close friend and neighbor, said she would be moving back to her hometown—about two hours away. I was surprised by the fear I felt at her announcement. What was this fear about? Slowly I worked my way toward the source.

A part of my history that loomed large in my mind was that of people coming into my life, becoming important supports, and then leaving. We moved far away from Grandpa. The numerous moves of my childhood and adolescence necessitated making new friends time and again, only to leave each friend within months or a few years. Dave appeared with a promise to stay, supported my life for many years, and then left.

After Dave, my new companions felt like critical supports for this new life. What I discovered now was that I was clinging to these new family members, much as a spider clings to its web in the wind. With Beth's announcement, I saw that one of these thick threads—a very important one—was giving way. I would be left once again. And fear reared its head.

As close neighbors, Beth and I had seen each other nearly daily, if only for a few minutes at a time, throughout all the years since Dave left for good. We kept up with each other's life on evening walks. We accompanied one another in sickness, worry, and joy. We knew and delighted in each other's children and their lives. We shared spur-of-the-moment dinners and outings. Beth was the one person who knew about the little details of my life. And now she was moving away, not so far that we would not see each other occasionally, but far enough that she could no longer provide daily support. I feared being once again so alone in life. I realized I couldn't rely on the center of my web to stay put.

I worked hard to let go of the fear. As I sat with the fear in silent prayer, I felt its power gradually diminish. As I remembered my own story—how in my time of despair I had again and again found important human connections—I drew courage and was able, before Beth's move, to return to trusting life.

After her move, we visited each other regularly. It was clear our friendship would continue, but in a new form. But then, barely six months later, one of my visits to her home showed me how tightly I was still clinging to my web vision of family. I discovered another old fear that had me holding tight.

Thanksgiving was approaching, and it seemed that I would be alone. Although Thanksgiving had been an important family gathering time for me throughout my adult life, I thought it would be all right to be alone this year. Still, I eagerly accepted an invitation to drive to Beth's new home the day after Thanksgiving for an overnight visit with her and her husband. And as Thanksgiving came closer, I was delighted to find myself invited to join in another friend's Thanksgiving dinner. But on Thanksgiving morning, as I bent over in a simple task, my back went out. Pain flooded in, and I was able to straighten up only with great difficulty. Eventually I made it to a phone to tell folks that I could not join them for dinner.

I spent long hours lying flat on my back. The pain was familiar. I had experienced it before, but not for several years. When the pain didn't ease, I found the muscle relaxants that had helped with earlier back troubles. Drugged, I eased onto my back and slept fitfully through the night.

The next morning I could rise more easily. If I walked carefully, I experienced only a little pain. Given this change, and my desire to be with friends, I decided to set out on the two-hour drive to Beth's. The trip went rather easily. I thought all was going to be okay as long as I was careful about how I moved. But after an hour of sitting on their porch, the pain returned with force when I tried to stand. Within a few hours I was unable to do anything but lie flat.

I am a houseguest from hell, I thought. I could barely raise my head to eat or drink. I couldn't manage a knife; others had to cut up food for me. I lay on my back on their living room floor with their cat curled up against me.

Still there were moments of fun. When a holiday special came on TV, Beth and her husband dragged a tall, antique, free-standing mirror into their living room. With careful calculations, they arranged it precisely so that it would reflect the TV show to me at my spot on the floor.

That evening I managed to climb the stairs to their guest bedroom before being flooded with worries about how I was to manage alone the next day. Could I drive myself home? If so, how would I get the suitcase into the house? I could hardly carry my purse. How would I manage food? Eventually I fell asleep and slept well.

The next morning, I managed to dress myself and negotiate the stairs. I decided to leave at once, while still in only moderate pain. I was able to drive home and walk into the house carrying only the critical toiletries. I discovered how to nudge a chair toward the refrigerator, sit on it and scoop some homemade soup from the refrigerator's bottom shelf into a lightweight bowl, and then lift the bowl into the microwave. I ate, lay down, and slept.

During the next several days of recovery, I thought back over my decision to make the trip. Why was it so important to be with my friends? I knew I could manage quite well on my own at home, even with debilitating back pain. Why was it so important to have people who cared for me around me?

A startling answer emerged. Having friends close, keeping them close, was proof that I was lovable. I had been using the people who cared for me to allay that old fear that I was unlovable. The realization filled me with grief. This was no way I wished to treat others, to honor their love. A prayer formed within me: "May I treat others as gift, with gratefulness. May I hold them lightly with palm stretched outward and open—not with a grasping hand." Week by week, I became more able to do so. I no longer found myself anxiously seeking out time with friends. These times just came and I savored them. When I caught any hint of clinging or grasping, I expressed my intent to treat friends as gifts and rested in that desire.

Other lessons with family quickly followed. Brett developed a non-Hodgkins form of lymphoma and underwent two four-week bouts of day-long IV-infusions of ritoxan as he and Ellie planned their wedding. I held them in wordless prayer, asking only for guidance in how to accompany them in this time. Six months later, Brett and Ellie had the marriage ceremony they dreamed of at the North Carolina coast surrounded by a new blend of family—mine, Dave's, and Ellie's. We celebrated Brett and Ellie's new life together while holding the knowledge that Brett's lymphoma could recur at any time.

Soon thereafter I faced a change in my relationship with Jeannene due to her moving far away. This time I felt no fear, no anxiety, no attempt to grasp or hold fast. There was love, deep appreciation for our time together, and a sense of real loss. For over five years she had been my spiritual director—through my beginning steps in faith, through illnesses, through discerning my own call to become a spiritual companion, through all my lessons with Mom, through Mom's dying, and through the many changes in my family. I had shared more of my inner self with her than anyone else. I felt a profound sense of loss, but also hopeful expectancy about what might lie ahead for us—hope, too, about what other gifts of family might be placed in my open hands.

Yet another vision of family began to open up. The threads of my web disappeared and I saw the people I have known immersed in the ocean of God's love.

This mysterious God holds each one of us as individuals, but also holds all of us—and all of creation—in connection with one another. Thomas Kelly's words resonate with this image: "God is the medium, the matrix, the focus, the solvent...." Some people are floating in this mystery; others are struggling or striving to move against the current. Always there is movement, the continuing flow of creativity and love that is God and the turbulent movement occasioned by our human flailing about in our fears and defenses.

The people closest around me are in flux. Sometimes two of us are side by side; later, we may drift apart. Sometimes we face one another, looking deeply into each other. At other times our backs are turned. Sometimes we hold hands and journey together until our hands part. New people come close to me, and some who were close depart.

My sense that Mom journeys with me beyond death led me to imagine that family members who have died remain in this ocean with the potential to come close and companion me beyond their deaths.

I suspected this conception of family would continue to evolve, and perhaps change in important ways. Letting go of fixed threads and including all of creation in my new vision, however, felt like big steps toward answering the question: "Who's family?" I found myself reliving so many scenes of surprising, life-enriching moments of interaction with "strangers" —and with other forms of creation new to me.

I recalled the woman standing in front of me in a long airport check-in line. After ten minutes of waiting, she turned to me with concern.

"I'm hoping I can make my flight and get home before my dad dies," she said.

After expressing hope for her to arrive in time, I said: "My dad died just a few months ago. It felt important to be with him then."

"But I don't know how to be with someone who is dying," she confessed.

For the next twenty minutes, as we slowly wended our way toward the ticket counter, we discussed ways to be with someone who is dying and her fears in all of this. Later, we found a place to sit together and continue our conversation as she awaited her flight. We parted with a hug, expressions of love, and hope for the time ahead of her.

I remembered, too, a few moments in Peru when nine of us fellow travelers had made our way by boat up the Mazan River, two days beyond any human habitation. On this clear, moon-lit night, we were camped on the banks of the river, within the Amazon jungle. Our guide had brought along his dad's hand-hewn dugout canoe, and we were taking turns canoeing at the confluence between the Mazan River and one of its tributaries. I paddled with our Peruvian guide and his wife away from camp and beyond all reach of the camp's sounds or firelight. As we moved in silence in the moonlight, suddenly two pink dolphins appeared beside us—a mother and calf, I thought. For the next several minutes, they "played" with us in a graceful dance that brought them close, appearing from beneath the water just beside our canoe, before darting away only to return once more. I felt such oneness with all around me—with the jungle, its night sounds, the moonlight and stars, the river, the dolphins, the near strangers within the canoe with me. Such oneness with "otherness," with all I had never experienced before.

Surely, I thought, my vision of family can expand to incorporate all such life-giving moments of connection.

An incident two and a half years after Mom's death helped me see just how far I had come in realizing that I am immersed in family, no matter what. It happened during a meeting with a woman to whom I had been offering spiritual direction for almost five years. One of her wounds was the death of her husband early in their marriage and the absence of a "life partner" in all the years since. This day her sense of aloneness and its pain was all she could talk about, even though she had close friends. After listening for quite a while, I gently asked:

"Are you really all alone?"

"Yes, and you are too," she heatedly replied. "Is there someone to greet you when you return to your home from work, or a trip?"

"No," I said.

"Do you have someone to talk with every night about the little happenings of your day?"

"No."

"Do you have someone for whom you are the center of their life?"

"No."

Each question she asked, I answered with a simple "no." But after several more questions, she took a pause and looked into my face.

"But I do not feel alone," I said.

"Yes, I know," she said with a sigh and a smile. "And I want that."

After she left, I went once more through the litany of questions she had asked me. She reminded me of myself at earlier points in my life, expressing not just what I desired, or hoped for, but *needed*. Gratefulness filled me, as once again I sent brief loving glances to God. For so long, I could only see and feel scarcity. Now I saw that I had been offered an abundance of family throughout my life, and always will be. In our essence, we all are loving kin.

My Song

"May I be the song uttered in my creation."

As the third anniversary of Mom's death approached, I began to understand more about these words. I had been thinking that they spoke of my desire to live ever more fully as my "true self" or "authentic self." Grounding in sacred mystery and giving up hiding seemed necessary ingredients for such a self. But the more specific content of my song had eluded me. Now I thought I might be hearing its melody. And I realized how my decision to retire had set in motion processes enabling this recognition.

Just a month before Mom's death, I had surprised myself by signing an agreement to retire in two years. I had previously planned to continue at Duke for at least ten more years, maybe many more. It wasn't that I was dissatisfied with my work as a teacher and researcher—not at all. I loved my profession. But being a professor had closed off other possibilities and placed heavy daily demands on my life. Perhaps it was time to create more space for the other activities that had already entered my life, and for whatever else might come. One event after another affirmed my decision.

One affirmation came as I talked with our new class of graduate students. I was to tell them about my career, especially about the questions I had pursued and how and why they changed. I had never done this before. But as I recounted the history of my research passions, a picture emerged and stayed with me. I saw myself wrapping a box that bulged with gifts, tying a big bow around the box, and placing it carefully on a shelf behind me. I then turned to face the unknown with open hands.

I completed my final year of teaching and then embarked upon a year of sabbatical leave. "Terminal sabbatical" was what my university called it—a name I hoped to prove wrong. For me it was time to ease gracefully into a new phase of life. During the first six months, I completed my research projects. During the second, I approached with some dread the task of clearing out my office and laboratory. How would I responsibly dispose of the "stuff" of thirty-four years of teaching, conducting research, editing a journal, serving on a multitude of committees, and meeting with students?

To my surprise, the task was enjoyable. I could give away most of my books to colleagues and students. My journals went to a group restocking libraries gutted by the tsunami in Asia. All the toys and children's furnishings used in my research went to daycare centers that served low-income children. What of my audio, video, and computer equipment was up-to-date found a home in other labs. I felt joy as I set each of these possessions free and they found new life elsewhere.

Going through all my research data—papers, video and audio tapes, CDs—proved less joyful and much more work, yet satisfying nevertheless. I handled each item, separating out those to be recycled, shredded, or kept. I became reacquainted with all the people who had worked with me as I once again saw their names. So many young students and assistants had passed through my lab, and my life, on the way to the rest of their lives.

Even all the hours spent shredding felt remarkably good. Shredding became a ritual that honored how I was putting this rewarding part of my life behind me and readying myself for whatever might come.

When I entered the newly emptied rooms, it felt like walking into a ghost land. The spirit of my research and teaching efforts, and of all the students who had sat and talked there, laughed and shed tears, still filled the rooms. I sat in the companionable silence and said my "thank-you's" for this part of life—and my "good-bye's."

The sabbatical year was anything but a spacious time, yet it prepared the way for a time to wait and listen. I started upon a year of feeling my way along in this next phase of life, feeling immensely privileged that I had the financial resources to take this step. For the first time in my life, I had long stretches of open space in my days—and I did not try to control their use. I called this time my "year of listening." I promised myself to not embark upon any major new endeavors. I would continue to make music with others, offer spiritual direction, write, visit my children, work within my church—all those things that already were part of my life. Would some of these activities naturally expand, contract, or disappear? I wanted to discover what entered on its own into the listening space I had created.

What first caught my attention was a steady stream of new invitations to offer hospitality. Two college roommates suddenly reappeared in my life—one just showing up on my doorstep, hoping to share life stories; another moving to my town. An acquaintance asked me to help her friend who was moving to town. A pastor asked me to spend some time with a woman who had visited our church and expressed concern about an operation her child was about to undergo. When I was our church's caregiver for the week, a member mentioned that a former member was returning to town for medical treatment of her MS and breast cancer and asked whether I could help arrange transportation and companionship for her medical appointments.

These and several more unexpected invitations came into my life, all within a span of just a few months. And I delighted in offering what I could in each case. It felt like parts of me were opening more fully to life—blooming.

It wasn't long before I realized that my offers of hospitality often led to something more. The words "being a companion" began to resonate with me. I thought of a companion as someone who faithfully shares the bread of everyday life with another over a period of months or years. For over six years I had offered spiritual direction to others, one form of being a companion. But now I found myself becoming a companion to several others without any mention of "spiritual direction."

Since the death of my marriage, I had become acquainted with a greater variety of people; and I had come to know several folks whom I thought of as ready companions to others. Both Doris and Beth were prime examples. They seemed so much more at ease than I with new people, knowing just what to say. I had never felt this way, except perhaps in my role as a spiritual director. In less circumscribed interactions, I habitually saw myself as more of a loner, sometimes a bit of a misfit, who yearned for others, like Doris and Beth, to companion me. It was only toward the end of my year of listening that I realized, with something like astonishment, that I was sharing the everyday lives of at least fourteen people—as a companion. I had never before envisioned this as a possible way of life for me. Could I be hearing, and singing, my song?

Each new person had come as I responded to an unexpected invitation. I had not tried to make these relationships happen or to control the form they took, how long they would last, or how they might nurture me. The familiar old feelings of striving, of trying to control, were mostly absent—as was the old neediness to do enough for others to prove myself lovable. I felt more like a spectator at my own life, watching with wonder what was unfolding. Also, I knew my delight in these new relationships. I felt joy, empathy, and love flowing out of me as I walked beside these people.

As I started to think about myself as a companion, that this might be my song, I began to realize that some of the elements of this song had been with me throughout my life.

My many attempts to control life and allay fear may have muted, or even distorted, its notes. But actually the willingness to share others' lives over an extended period, to listen attentively, to accompany them in joy and sorrow, and to aid when help was called for—these themes could be found throughout my life.

As I took a long walk in the woods one day, thinking back over all the invitations of the past few months, I suddenly saw similarities between how I had approached research for over thirty years and what I now called being a companion. I fell to the ground in laughter. How could this be! How had I failed to see this before?

Scenes flooded in of me as a twenty-five-year-old crawling around on the floor with my fifty-plus-year-old mentor. We did this as we designed each new research setting. We were trying to imagine, as best we could, how crawling infants might experience it. And even before trying to design a setting to test our ideas about what guided their crawling, we would spend hours in infants' homes or public spaces, carefully observing when and where they moved.

I realized anew how experiential, how inductive, I had been in research. I had never followed the strategy of deducing from a theory what I should see in infants' or toddlers' behavior—the strategy most highly valued in the institutions of my training and employment. Instead, I had tried to see the world through the eyes and limbs of the young child. I wanted to understand how a child's new experiences worked together with his or her present way of functioning so as to yield a new step of development. And, in this way, I accompanied children in one after another developmental step during their first three years of life.

A related insight came during a dinner to mark and celebrate my retirement. At dessert time, a colleague read from statements she had gathered from several of my former students. As I listened to how they described me as a mentor, I suddenly realized the similarity to some of the themes of "being a companion." They said I had listened closely as they framed their research questions and helped them refine their questions and learn more about what they were seeking. Then I had worked with them step-by-step as they developed their research methods, affirming some moves and questioning others. Once they had their results, I celebrated with them and prodded them to delve further into the implications of their findings. Of course, it was a retirement event where kind words and stretches of the "truth" are to be expected. But I recognized myself in what they were saying, and saw for the first time the connection between my mentoring of students and being a companion.

I also realized how my academic life was an important player in some of the new companioning relationships. I had taught about phenylketonuria all my academic life, as an accessible example of how genes and environmental influences are inextricably intertwined in human development. Now I was using all I had taught as I companioned the parents of a baby with this disorder. Similarly, I had conducted research with very-prematurely-born infants and their parents for over fifteen years, relating medical problems to patterns of parent-infant interaction that helped shape infant development. I was able to use all of this anew when a friend initiated a series of conversations on topics occasioned by the premature birth of her grandson. As this baby's life hung in the balance over many months, we talked about the nature of prayer, how to make medical decisions, why there is no way to know how this child will develop if he survives, how to accompany her daughter in this time, and the beauty that exists even amidst so much pain.

Finding these threads of continuity led me to look even farther back in time, and review all I knew of my life. Again and again, I found ways I had tried to companion others: my attempts to mother my mother from early in life; my efforts over so many years to live with Dave in more intimate ways; my being on call to meet with women who had miscarried; my delight in mothering my children; the ten years of walking with the woman who suffered severe mental illness; my multiple stints as Director of Graduate Studies within my department, when I accompanied students through their professional crises, conflicts and celebrations; the roles I had taken on in my church—Elder, caregiver, chair of Personnel Committee.

I now realized for the first time how I had naturally reached out to companion others throughout my life. I had tried to give to others what I so wanted for myself, what I responded to as a precious gift. For many years those offerings were intermixed with my own neediness. But in recent years, I had become increasingly able to freely offer this form of love, not needing or trying to get anything in return.

So, had I finally discovered my song? I now thought that at least part of my song was to be a faithful companion to others, and that I had been singing themes of this song throughout my life. What was new was that I had come to recognize the song and to sing it more freely and clearly.

"I will restore to you the years that the locust hath eaten." Jeannene had offered these words to me over seven years earlier, at the end of our very first meeting for spiritual direction. She asked me to wait a moment while she searched for the verse of scripture (Joel 2.25, KJV) that had come to her as we talked. These were the words I left with, and they have stayed with me ever since.

At first I held them as a promise for the future. Then, when I moved more fully into my new life of faith and unexpected joy, I thought the promise had been fulfilled. Wasn't this new life I had begun around age fifty-seven a replacement for my former life—the one with the locusts?

Years later, shortly after Mom's death, I came to a different understanding of the promise. My former life was not to be dismissed. I then accepted and held my entire life journey with gratitude. It all was just my particular path toward these later years that I called my "whole new life."

But now, I discovered that there was even more than I had ever imagined in the promise. Finding the themes of my song interwoven throughout my life transformed how I viewed my entire journey. Not just the years since my discovery of faith and joy, but all my life had become a "whole new life." It all had been restored.

Simply Being

It is now eighteen years since my old life began to crumble around me. So what do I now know about "simply being," these words that have been ringing in me for almost eight years?

Two years ago, I thought I had a great deal more to say. The developmental scientist in me kicked in right after I heard the strains of my song. Questions began to whirl within me, demanding answers. Where does this melody of love come from? How is it shaped by factors both inside and outside me? Where am I now? What lies ahead? What is simply being?

I tried to put these questions aside when I began my silent retreat that year. I wanted to be open to whatever the time would offer. And within two days, some surprising new words emerged—"abandon oneself to love." On the third day, however, all the questions returned with a vengeance. During centering prayer, scenes of me as a flute floating within a sea of love began showing up. Occasionally I grasped at the images, working with them, trying to find answers. But when I caught myself at this, I returned to my sacred word and my intent to let the images just be.

Outside of the prayer times, however, I found myself repeatedly thinking about these scenes and struggling to find answers. I realize now that I wasn't holding the images given in prayer receptively. I tried to wring answers from them. And by the seventh day, I thought I had. I began to write "What is Simply Being?" I wanted to offer a blueprint, or perhaps a road map, that explained in more general, abstract terms where I had been and where I was going.

I continued working on this writing after I returned home, and eventually offered it to my writing coach. She said little at first. But after we had worked through another round of editing the earlier chapters, we turned to this one. What I took away from her comments was something like: "You sound pretty sure of yourself, as if you have arrived, maybe even reached Nirvana!" That took me aback. I was full of wonder about what I had lived, and what lay ahead felt even more mysterious. How had I conveyed such a different impression? I set to work, tweaking this and that paragraph, hoping to get a new, improved version to her before I left for my next annual silent retreat. But something stopped me. I didn't know what or why. Suddenly I felt a nudge to put the writing away, and I did.

I entered the retreat time without any of the questions or answers begging for attention. I brought my computer, just in case I felt led to write. But I never did. I fasted from almost all words, either written or spoken.

The second evening, we watched a video of Thomas Keating talking about centering prayer. I delighted in finding some words that lit up for me. "Spirit grasps your will," he said. "Yes," my heart responded. These words fit some of my experience of prayer. Keating went on to describe how prayer changed as Spirit grasped your will more and more tightly. I dutifully took notes about this sequence, even though these words did not readily connect with my experience. Perhaps this was what lay ahead, I thought.

The next morning, during our first communal prayer period, all was much like it often had been, a deep sense of stillness and open presence. It felt indeed as if Spirit had grasped me and was holding me in some place beyond my more usual way of being. During the next time of prayer, however, I found myself trying to name what was happening. Was this prayer type x, y, or z? Then I realized how hard I was working at being more receptive so that these prayer types might emerge. I was striving, trying to place myself within Keating's conceptual system—and I was trying to "progress," whatever that meant.

How had I gotten here? This was counter to all I understood about centering prayer. I realized how tempting it was for me to grasp for a conceptual system of understanding, even during prayer where I knew my deeper desire for simple open presence. In subsequent prayer times I was able to return to my intent to be open to "whatever."

During my daily walks I found myself thinking back over the prior year, reliving several events. I saw how again and again, in different ways, I had grasped for analytical understanding. And each time I had somehow been led back to simple open presence. For much of the year, for example, I had wrestled with concepts about Jesus. It began as an attempt to answer a quintessentially grasping question: Who is Jesus? Within six months, my question somehow had changed into Jesus': "Who do you say I am?" I had let go of attempts to read and reason my way through theological arguments to some "correct" answer and had come to simply stand in the presence of Jesus, giving my heart's response to his question. I saw that my answer had changed, deepened, over the years, and become harder and harder to express in words. I became able to see how others' answers might differ and yet be right for them.

I had participated for six months in a Contemplative Wisdom School offered by Cynthia Bourgeault, in large measure because I thought it promised to give me more understanding of what Jesus had actually done and said and what his early followers believed about him. During the first week-long residency, I struggled mightily to understand the conceptual system offered — the cosmovision that Bourgeault suggested was a useful context for understanding Jesus' life and teachings. I left frustrated that so much of this vision was beyond my experience, and that some of what I had experienced didn't seem to fit.

A month later, at a Shalem gathering, I found myself unexpectedly sitting in front of a large reproduction of Rublev's icon of the trinity for an hour or more at a time. It spoke to me, in a way beyond all words, of the flow of self-giving love among the three angelic figures. The hand of the left-most figure, the one I took to be Jesus, seemed to reach out to me, beckoning me into the flow. My heart answered "yes."

By the second residency with Bourgeault, barely a month later, I had observed my earlier grasping after analytical understanding. This time, I just let her words flow over me, remaining responsive to whatever spoke to me. Much did. For the remainder of the school, I treated our readings and her teaching sessions as times of *lectio divina*, listening for where and how Spirit was speaking to me through these words. And toward the end of the final residency, I came upon another reproduction of the Rublev trinity icon tucked away in a vacant room I had wandered into. I stood before it transfixed, sensing once again the invitation to be one with this flow of love.

After reliving how I had come to trust my heart response to Jesus, I thought about what I had written the prior year in "What is simply being?" I saw my striving, how hard I had worked to come up with a general model that fit pretty well what I had already lived and that also told me what lay ahead. I had wrestled partial answers from the images and words that had emerged during the prior year's retreat. I knew then, at once, that I was to let go of the need for a neat conceptual scheme to offer myself, or anyone else. I was to return once again to "a path of unknowing." Others may be called to offer conceptualizations — but I wasn't, not now.

This path of unknowing was not unlike where I had arrived during my thirty-year quest to understand early human development. I had observed hundreds of very young children in research settings — in the United States, Brazil, Norway, and Papua New Guinea. This opportunity had enabled me to highlight some wonders of young children's behavior, to point out previously overlooked ways of acting and demonstrate how they yield valuable new experiences. Sometimes I could establish a set developmental order in which new behaviors emerged, even when children grew up in markedly different cultural contexts.

Occasionally, I was able to demonstrate that a specific set of experiences was one of the factors influencing a subsequent development. At times, I could persuasively place my findings within a more complex model of developmental change, like that of developmental systems theory. Never, however, was I able to catch hold of the actual process of developmental change. I could theorize about how a change took place, but at heart it remained for me unknown.

I remembered my delight in finding words by physicist and astronomer Chet Raymo that expressed my own sense of how mystery continued to permeate and surround my understanding of early development. In his book, *Honey from Stone,* Raymo discusses at length our current scientific knowledge about how snowflakes are created, and then writes:

"I have a friend who speaks of knowledge as an island in a sea of mystery...We live in our partial knowledge as the Dutch live on polders claimed from the sea...We dredge up soil from the bed of mystery and build ourselves room to grow. And still the mystery surrounds us. It laps our shores. It permeates the land. Scratch the surface of knowledge and mystery bubbles up like a spring."

I saw how well these words also fit the story I have told.

I can extract from this story several aspects of my movement toward a radically different way of living. I came to trust life instead of hiding behind barriers and clinging to my old strategies of control—those old lessons. Trust grew, deepened, as I experienced the unfolding of my own journey. Love grew, too. Each experience that increased my trust led to an even greater outpouring of love and gratefulness for the mysterious loving presence I call "God." If I envision myself as a flute, I see that I became increasingly freer of the wastepaper of old fears and attachments that distort the flow of God's breath of life through me. I discovered more and more ways I try to seize control in life, and something enabled me to let them go, one by one. I became more present in the moment and able to sense more of what it holds. I envision this as sensing the ebb and flow of the currents of the sea of love in which I exist. And I became more willing and able to align myself with these currents—to float more continuously in the sea's various weathers. I increasingly sensed the deep interconnectedness of all life, that we all are kin. I heard the strains of "my song," my distinctive way of offering love, and found myself singing more freely. I became more able to show up as my "authentic self" and trust that it's enough to just be me, that there's no need to hide. Fear largely disappeared; joy, peacefulness, freedom stand in its place.

I can point to these changes, but I can go no further with any confidence. I cannot weave them into an orderly progression of stages in my journey. Nor can I explain how the changes came about. I have recounted the circumstances surrounding each and the order in which they occurred, but why they happened just when they did and how each came about remain a mystery to me.

In the living of my story, I have been building the polder of simply being. My island expanded and hopefully will continue to grow. But, "scratch the surface of knowledge and mystery bubbles up like a spring." And as my landmass grew, so did the shoreline along which I encountered sacred mystery. The steps in my journey did not capture or tame mystery. Rather they added new dimensions to my awareness of it—new appreciation for the wonder of human life and our immersion within the infinite sea of divine love and creativity.

I now tread this path of unknowing, listening once again to the words that first emerged two years ago amidst all my grasping for a conceptual analysis of simply being—"abandon oneself to love." During the past year the words "in and of the flow" have joined the chorus. I am not sure when or how this phrase first emerged. But I know it evokes the image of Rublev's trinity icon that speaks to me so forcefully about the invitation to join in the flow of divine love.

Throughout this year's silent retreat, these two phrases reverberated in me—while hiking, eating, falling asleep, arising.... Daily I found myself walking and sitting beside a stream in the park adjacent to the retreat house. I would start where the boulder-strewn water divided, encircling an island from which I could watch the water stream over and around rocks—all around me. Sometimes I envisioned the surging water as the flow of love and the boulders as our many forms of grasping. The merged streams soon formed a large placid mill pond—so still that it mirrored all the life around it. Water bugs punctuated its surface, jumping from place to place in a dance of life. The water seemed to throw up a strip of land in its middle that gave life to an abundance of plants. Butterflies, birds, and dragonflies flew about, landing on the plant life. I thought of this nurturance of life as the fruits of unobstructed, or less obstructed, flow. As I walked farther along the millpond's edge, the water precipitously shattered as it plunged over a steep dam, only to gather again into a stream of rapids, swirling eddies, and more gentle flows. Perhaps a quarter of a mile downstream, it took on the form of two calm pools connected by a narrow channel.

As I sat beside the water in all its forms, I thought of three very different stances I could take. I could observe the stream from outside it—an observer watching a subject and trying to analyze it. I could be "in" it—floating, struggling, tubing, swimming...in direct contact but still somewhat separate from the flow. Or I could be "of" the stream, indistinguishable in my essence from it—participating in its life from the inside. Suddenly the phrase "in and of the flow" took on new meaning and merged with "abandon oneself to love. The words of John O'Donohue's poem "Fluent" floated into consciousness: "I would love to live as a river flows, carried by the surprise of its own unfolding." I heard it as a longing to live the path of unknowing from within the flow. My heart, my body, my whole being seemed to shout "yes."

I suspect these words and scenes keep arising because they speak of something in process within me.

Such an abandoning of oneself is what I believe Thomas Greene writes about as the deepest essence of floating in the sea of God's mercy. Two years ago I found his revised edition of *When the Well Runs Dry*. I bought it because it was in the first edition that I had found the image of floating that spoke to me about simply being right after Mom's death. As I read the new edition, I realized that he is talking about the essence of floating as when we have no will of our own. We have allowed the will of the water to become our own. There is only God's will.

Words like "surrendering your will" can be hard for us since they often carry the connotation of subjugation to an external force. But I, and I think Thomas Greene, envision this abandonment differently. It is a surrender to, and flowering of, what is deepest and truest within us—that of sacred mystery incarnate in us. We let go of all that separates us from the flow of divine love both within and beyond us. We live and act from that of God in us—in harmony with the sacred mystery that surrounds us and holds all in existence.

The image of me as a flute floating in the sea of God's love changed in a critical way. In abandoning myself to love I would no longer be striving to align my separate self with the ebb and flow of its currents, trying to play the music of God's score. Rather these currents, those both inside and outside me, would be shaping my breath and finger movements so that God is making music through my distinctive flute.

I suspect this abandoning is not something I can make happen, no matter how much I desire it. A long line of Christian contemplatives talk of it as sheer grace. Although how we surrender to the flow of God's love is mystery, perhaps we can catch glimpses afterwards of moments when it has happened.

Thomas Greene suggests that it is the "accidents" in his life that have given him a little taste of this final surrender. Some of the most important times for him and the seminarians he was guiding were those when everything he had planned for their outings went "wrong." He talks about feeling like a spectator observing the unfolding of his life.

I, too, have at times felt like a spectator, especially during my year of listening, when unexpected relationships emerged. And perhaps I have caught brief glimpses of this when new words, images, or insights floated into consciousness, filling me with awe. Or when I just knew, without knowing how or why, what decision to make for Mom's care. When words simply flow out of me without forethought during spiritual direction. When I experience at-oneness with all about me, as with the pink dolphins and the Amazon jungle. I suspect we all have been offered tastes of this abandonment, even though we may not be able to recognize them at the time.

So what am I offering with my story? Not a conceptualization of the spiritual journey. Not the full meaning of these words "simply being." As a "recovering control addict" I may be able to walk beside you for a while as you, too, break free from your addictions. You may find points of contact between my steps and your own, affirmations of some of your movements and warnings about possible missteps. Hopefully you will find reasons to hope, the courage to trust, and a vision to bring into possibility what you may have thought unimaginable. In my story, too, you may find some useful books, ways of praying, or forms of spiritual companionship.

So many valuable companions—books, people, and groups— have met me in my journey that I can readily join in Teresa of Avila's exclamation: "Through the flight of these others, we also make bold to fly." Perhaps my story will help you fly, in your own way. I haven't felt much like a flyer—more like a plodding, slow learner. But as a researcher of early human development, I know something about how slowness in change can help us catch glimpses of all the steps involved. Esther Thelen, a theorist of developmental process, first helped me appreciate slowness as we talked about her efforts to understand motor development. For her, the human infant, who often takes some ten to twelve months to walk alone, was ideal for studying the processes involved in walking—much better than say a colt or calf that becomes adept in only a day or two. So sharing my slow steps toward simply being may help you envision the processes at work, and the possibilities for flight.

I offer you, too, the words and scenes that keep repeating in me, inviting me—drawing me—into an intimacy with sacred mystery beyond all words, images, or concepts.

I end with one more vision of abandoning oneself to love.

A Tale of Endings and Beginnings

It is the morning of the last full day of my annual retreat. The whirlpool image from my childhood emerged again—but in a totally transformed form. It came as the words "abandon oneself to love" rang within me. I saw myself alone in a whirlpool, but now it was a swirl of love. I was being drawn in some mysterious way into its very vortex, into love itself. And I wanted to be drawn.

Later in the day, after I wrote about this new vision and the invitation to abandon myself to love, I thought something important—some new learning—had reached a point of completion.

I decided to take a final "exercise walk" around the retreat grounds. So I took off on my customary path down to the lake, a well-maintained gravel road. I bowed to the two young deer studying me as I made my way to the water, and then gazed upon and bowed to the lake. The bowing was an acknowledgement of God in the other, and an expression of gratefulness. I then walked up a more overgrown path back toward the driveway that looped around the retreat house. I made my way to the cemetery I had visited daily. I would start from there, I thought, and then circle the retreat house two or three times for my exercise.

When I reached the cemetery, however, I saw the path that went beyond it, a path that I remember being told went toward the road that we had taken on our way to the retreat house. I started down the path, thinking it would give me a longer walk. As I heard the traffic noise in the distance, I decided that going to the road would be a fine way to mark the ending of this time. I would bow to it and its busyness to express my readiness to depart, carrying with me the transformed whirlpool image.

I arrived at the road and bowed. But as I retraced my steps, another path I hadn't seen before beckoned. This one was even more overgrown. I followed the trail, wondering where it would lead. I felt more alone in the woods than ever before, and the path kept becoming more overgrown, narrower, and harder to detect. I had to step over tree trunks and around low-hanging branches. Still, I kept finding stones that seemed to mark the way. Something kept drawing me onward. I remembered the words of one of our leaders, asking us to not wander too far without letting someone know where we were. Was I going too far? Might I get lost? What would happen if I tripped and sprained or broke something? Would help come? All these thoughts that cautioned against proceeding arose, but quickly left. Something was drawing me.

When the path became even harder to detect, I could look ahead and catch a glimpse of water through the trees. This path, too, led to the lake that I had bowed to at least once a day. But it was a different route. One I hadn't traveled before. One harder to detect. One that was slippery with dew, mud, and leaves.

Suddenly, this path seemed like the new whirlpool image, drawing me deeper and deeper into love. Then my eyes lit upon a small stone at my feet—a piece of bright white quartz. It stood out on the path and brought me to a stop. I picked it up as I often pick up pieces of nature that seem to speak to me. Here was a glimmer of brightness amidst all the shade. I thought: *Could this be like a spiritual consolation as one traveled what the mystics talk of as "the dark night" to union with love?*

I walked on. The path sloped sharply downward, toward the lake. It became still narrower, and even more slippery. But I made my way ahead, step by slow, careful step. Then I saw that the trail of stones I was following led right into the lake. *Yes, this was a path into something new and unknown — a something that drew me. Something I yearned to become immersed within.*

Three large flat stones rose partially above the water's surface, and led progressively farther into the lake. I made my way to the first. As I came close, I saw that the water deepened quickly. Was it safe to step onto it? I wanted to. I saw a stick leaning against a nearby tree and lifted it up, only to find it still rooted in the ground. But I could use it to brace myself as I stepped onto the first stone. *There were aids in this path, aids provided by others who had traveled this way before me.* The stone held steady. Then I put one foot on the second stone. It tipped, but I could balance myself carefully upon the two stones and look deep into the lake. All my being felt drawn toward this mystery, and I wanted to be drawn.

Then as I looked into the lake I saw nearby, but too far for me to retrieve it, a beer can resting on the lake's floor. All of a sudden this path didn't seem so other-worldly. Here was something very much a part of everyday, ordinary life. *Am I being drawn to love's vortex within my quite ordinary life?*

I bowed once more to the lake, deeply, and then stepped back on its shore. I replaced the stick, for someone else to use. And as I made my way up the steep part of the path, I found another stick that I could use to help draw myself up. *Yes, what is needed will be given.* When the path began to level out, I placed this stick against a tree, for someone else to find.

A bit farther up the trail, another stone caught my attention. I picked it up, an ordinary dull gray stone but with a bright gray portion emerging seamlessly, like a blossom, from its center. *Was this a symbol of God blooming in me, and potentially in all of everyday, ordinary life?*

By now I was sort of dancing, or prancing, in response to my joy and gratitude about the messages of this walk. It felt like a time of *lectio divina*. Only the text was not in the words of scripture but in what the Celtic Christian tradition calls God's book of creation.

A bit farther along in my prancing—perhaps I was feeling a bit special, or holy—a very green acorn in the path caught my eye. I picked it up. *This is me, a very green acorn. An ordinary person being drawn lovingly by God, and watered gently along the way in order that she might bloom a bit.* A few tears fell amidst my laughter at how I am taught daily about myself—about humility.

Still smiling, I made my way to the cemetery. As I approached, I saw dew on a patch of grass, sparkling like precious jewels in the sunlight. I touched my fingers to the jewels and made the sign of the cross on my forehead—the sign of my baptism. And then, I passed the woman who had sat beside me all week in silent prayer. She was making her way along the same path I had just traveled. We exchanged smiles and bows, and moved on.

I felt the push to write just as soon as the retreat house came into view. Write it down, Carol. Honor it. Bow to it. Share it. And most of all remember it, and live into it.

Endings are beginnings.
Love trumps fear.
Abandon oneself to love.
Simply be.

Acknowledgements

I am especially indebted to my children Brett and Lisa, my mother Doris Osterhout, my long-term spiritual companions Jeannene Wiseman, the Rev. J. Mark Davidson, and Sr. Joanna Walsh, FCJ; and my friends Beth McArthur, Doris Tippens, Sandy Milroy Jens, and Barbara Lang. Each has lovingly walked beside me in this eighteen-year odyssey. My children and former husband read earlier drafts, clarified points, and gave their blessings to sharing my version of our family story. The Shalem Institute for Spiritual Formation and the Shalem Society for Contemplative Leadership were key influences in my exploration of "faith." Contemplative Outreach offered guidance in centering prayer and the ten-day silent retreats I write of. The Carolina Meadows retirement community provided invaluable support during my mother's last years of life. Thanks, too, to my church home (the Church of Reconciliation), to the Wild Geese (my peer group of spiritual directors), and to my directees who have further nurtured my faith—it always flows both ways.

Carol Henderson—writing coach, mentor, and friend— patiently and creatively guided me toward less academic ways of writing and to finding even more meaning in what I had lived. Members of her Thursday Evening Writing Group also helped enliven my story-telling. Beatrice Bruteau, Tilden Edwards, Catherine Gibson, Nancy Oglesby, Katie Ricks, Patience Robbins, Kate Vosecky, and Larry Williams provided helpful comments on earlier drafts and encouragement to continue. Finally, I am grateful for all the insightful writers and writings I have encountered on this journey.

Endnotes

So many writers have traveled with me on this journey. I list here the full reference for the books, articles, and poems I have mentioned and/or quoted from. For some of these authors, and others that I have referred to only by name, I also list a few of their books that have aided me.

Adams, Richard, *Watership Down* (New York: Avon Books, 1975). The Bigwig quote is from p.61; the quote of Fiver, the visionary, from p.60.

Bourgeault, Cynthia, *Centering Prayer and Inner Awakening* (Cambridge, MA.: Cowley, 2004); *Mystical Hope: Trusting in the Mercy of God* (Boston, MA.: Cowley, 2001); *The Wisdom Jesus* (Boston, MA.: Shambhala, 2008); *The Wisdom Way of Knowing: Reclaiming an Ancient Tradition to Awaken the Heart* (San Francisco, CA.: Jossey-Bass, 2003).

Brooke, Avery, *Finding God in the World: Reflections on a Spiritual Journey* (Boston, MA.: Cowley, 1994).

Brussat, Frederic & Brussat, Mary Ann, *Spiritual Literacy: Reading the Sacred in Everyday Life* (New York: Scribner, 1996). The section on faith appears on pp.152-153.

Bruteau, Beatrice, *The Easter Mysteries* (New York: Crossroad, 1995). The section on spiritual striving appears on pp.91-115; the Merton quote, on p.117.

Bruteau, Beatrice, *Radical Optimism: Practicing Spirituality in an Uncertain World* (Boulder, CO.: Sentient, 2002).

Buechner, Frederick, *Telling Secrets* (New York: HarperCollins, 1991).

Catherine of Siena, *The Dialogue*, trans. Suzanne Noffke (New York: Paulist Press, 1980).

Chittister, Joan D., *The Rule of Benedict* (New York: Crossroad, 1992).

Edwards, Tilden, *Living in the Presence: Spiritual Exercises to Open Your Life to the Awareness of God* (New York: HarperCollins, 1987) and *Living Simply through the Day: Spiritual Survival in a Complex Age* (New York: Paulist Press, 1998).

Gibbons, Kate, *Ellen Foster* (Chapel Hill, NC.: Algonquin Books, 1987). Ellen's unhappy Christmas with her aunt appears on pp.104-110.

Green, Thomas H., *When the Well Runs Dry: Prayer Beyond the Beginnings* (Notre Dame, IN: Ave Maria Press, 1979). The image of floating in the sea of God's mercy is discussed on pp.142-149. First Revised Edition (Notre Dame, IN: Ave Maria Press, 1998). Discussion of will and floating appears on pp.165-167; being a spectator at one's life's unfolding, on pp.156-157; and the "accidents" of one's life, on p.169.

Guenther, Margaret, *Toward Holy Ground: Spiritual Directions for the Second Half of Life* (Boston, MA.: Cowley, 1995). Reflections on meaning of "family" appear on pp.19-47.

Hafiz, *The Gift: Poems by Hafiz*, trans. Daniel Ladinsky (New York: Penguin, 1999). The poem excerpt quoted is from p.203.

Hall, Thelma, *Too Deep for Words: Rediscovering Lectio Divina* (New York: Paulist Press, 1988).

Hayes, Edward, *Prayers for a Planetary Pilgrim: A Personal Manual for Prayer and Ritual* (Leavenworth, KS.: Forest of Peace Publishing, 1989).

Heschel, Abraham, *God in Search of Man: A Philosophy of Judaism* (New York: Noonday Press, 1955). Quotation about sensing God is from p.83.

Keating, Thomas, *Intimacy with God* (New York: Crossroad, 1994); *Invitation to Love: The Way of Christian Contemplation* (New York: Continuum, 2002); *Manifesting God* (New York: Lantern Books, 2005); *Open Mind, Open Heart: The Contemplative Dimension of the Gospel* (New York: Continuum, 1999).

Kelly, Thomas R., *A Testament of Devotion* (New York: Harper & Brothers, 1941). Quotation taken from the chapter entitled "The Blessed Community."

May, Gerald G., *The Dark Night of the Soul* (New York: HarperCollins, 2004). Quotation about the "bad" and "good" is from p.1.

May, Gerald G., *The Awakened Heart: Opening Yourself to the Love you Need* (New York: HarperCollins, 1991) and *Will and Spirit: A Contemplative Psychology* (New York: HarperCollins, 1982).

May, Gerald G., The quote appearing at the start of my book is widely attributed on the internet to Gerald May and often cited as appearing in his book *Simply Sane: The Spirituality of Mental Health* (New York: Crossroad, 1997), but I have been unable to find the quote in this book or his other books. The words, however, are so congruent with Gerald May's writings and my experience of him as a mentor that I, too, think they are likely his.

Merton, Thomas, *New Seeds of Contemplation* (New York: New Directions, 1961). Quotation about false self is from p.35.

Merton, Thomas, *Contemplative Prayer* (New York: Doubleday, Image Books Ed., 1996); *The Intimate Merton: His Life from His Journals*, ed. Patrick Hart & Jonathan Montaldo (New York: HarperCollins, 1999); *The Seven Storey Mountain* (New York: Harcourt Brace and Co., 1948).

Newell, J. Phillip, *The Book of Creation: An Introduction to Celtic Spirituality* (New York: Paulist Press, 1999). Quotation about sensing God is from p.70.

Newell, J. Phillip, *Celtic Benediction: Morning and Night Prayer* (Grand Rapids, MI.: William B. Eerdmans Publishing Co., 2000); *Christ of the Celts: The Healing of Creation* (San Francisco, CA.: Jossey-Bass, 2008); *Listening for the Heartbeat of God: A Celtic Spirituality* (New York: Paulist Press, 1997).

Norris, Kathleen, *Amazing Grace: A Vocabulary of Faith* (New York: Riverhead Books, 1998) and *The Cloister Walk* (New York: Riverhead Books, 1987).

Nouwen, Henri J.M., *Return of the Prodigal Son: A Story of Homecoming* (New York: Doubleday, 1992). The older son's reaction appears on pp.67-76.

Nouwen, Henri J.M., *The Inner Voice of Love: A Journey Through Anguish to Freedom* (New York: Doubleday, 1996). Chapter entitled "Receive all the Love that Comes to You" is pp.55-56.

Nouwen, Henri J.M., *With Open Hands* (Notre Dame, IN.: Ave Maria Press, 1995).

O'Donohue, John, *Conamara Blues* (New York: Harper/Collins, 2001). The poem *Fluent* appears on p.23.

Raymo, Chet, *Honey from Stone: A Naturalist's Search for God* (Saint Paul, MN.: Hungry Mind Press, 1997). Quotation about an island in a sea of mystery is from pp.58-59.

Rule of the Society of Saint John the Evangelist (Boston, MA.: Cowley, 1994).

St. John of the Cross, *John of the Cross: Selected Writings*, trans. and ed. Kieran Kavanaugh, O.C.D. (New York: Paulist Press, 1987).

St. Teresa of Avila, *The Interior Castle*, from *The Collected Works of St. Teresa of Avila*, vol. 2, trans. Kieran Kavanaugh, O.C.D. & Otilio Rodriguez, O.C.D. (Washington, DC.: ICS Publications, 1980). Quotation about making bold to fly is from p.314.

Smith, Huston. The ideas I attributed to Smith during my talk with Duke students came from a talk he gave at Duke University, October 2000.

Steindle-Rast, Brother David, *Gratefulness: The Heart of Prayer* (New York: Paulist Press, 1984).

Thibault, Jane, "Mourning Pages," *Weavings* 15 (March/April 2000), 29-38.

Circle Books

Circle is a symbol of infinity and unity. It's part of a growing list of imprints, including o-books.net and zero-books.net.

Circle Books aims to publish books in Christian spirituality that are fresh, accessible, and stimulating.

Our books are available in all good English language bookstores worldwide. If you can't find the book on the shelves, then ask your bookstore to order it for you, quoting the ISBN and title. Or, you can order online—all major online retail sites carry our titles.

To see our list of titles, please view www.Circle-Books.com, growing by 80 titles per year.

Authors can learn more about our proposal process by going to our website and clicking on Your Company > Submissions.

We define Christian spirituality as the relationship between the self and its sense of the transcendent or sacred, which issues in literary and artistic expression, community, social activism, and practices. A wide range of disciplines within the field of religious studies can be called upon, including history, narrative studies, philosophy, theology, sociology, and psychology. Interfaith in approach, Circle Books fosters creative dialogue with non-Christian traditions.

And tune into MySpiritRadio.com for our book review radio show, hosted by June-Elleni Laine, where you can listen to authors discussing their books.

MySpiritRadio